OBERIU

»»»»»»»»» «««««««««

OBERIU

An Anthology
of Russian Absurdism

EDITED BY EUGENE OSTASHEVSKY
TRANSLATED FROM THE RUSSIAN

NORTHWESTERN UNIVERSITY PRESS
EVANSTON, ILLINOIS

»»»»»»»»» «««««««««

Northwestern University Press
www.nupress.northwestern.edu

Translated from the Russian by Eugene Ostashevsky and Matvei Yankelevich with
contributions by Thomas Epstein, Ilya Bernstein, and Genya Turovskaya.

Printed in the United States of America

10 9 8 7 6 5 4 3 2 1

ISBN 0–8101-2293–6

Library of Congress Cataloging-in-Publication Data

OBERIU : an anthology of Russian absurdism / edited by Eugene Ostashevsky.
    p. cm.
    "Translated from the Russian by Eugene Ostashevsky and Matvei Yankelevich
with contributions by Thomas Epstein, Ilya Bernstein, and Genya Turovskaya"—
T.p. verso.
    Includes bibliographical references.
    ISBN 0-8101-2293-6 (pbk. : alk. paper)
    1. Obériu—Literary collections. 2. Russian literature—20th century—
Translations into English. 3. Absurd (Philosophy)—Literary collections.
4. Literature, Experimental—Soviet Union. I. Ostashevsky, Eugene.
II. Yankelevich, Matvei. III. Epstein, Thomas, 1954– . IV. Bernstein, Ilya.
V. Turovskaya, Genya.
PG3213.O24 2005
891.7080384—dc22

                                                              2005023271

♾ The paper used in this publication meets the minimum requirements of the
American National Standard for Information Sciences—Permanence of Paper for
Printed Library Materials, ANSI Z39.48–1992.

In memory of Joseph Ostashevsky, 1945–2003

»»» CONTENTS ««»

Yakov Druskin

»»» ACKNOWLEDGMENTS «««

The editor and translators wish to express their gratitude to Mitch and Linda Wycheslavzoff, Nikita Zabolotsky, Aleksandr Oleinikov, Lidia Druskina, and Ellendea Teasley for permission to publish these translations. Luba Ostashevsky, Galina Dursthoff, Steve Curry, and Mikhail Meilakh provided assistance in copyright matters. Andrew Wachtel helped us place the manuscript with Northwestern University Press, where Anne Gendler and Lori Meek Schuldt copyedited it. We have also incorporated editorial suggestions by Elena Bonner, Inna Giter, Michael Goldman-Donnelly, Susan Harris, Branislav Jakovljevic, Susanne Fusso, Paul LaFarge, Andrei Ustinov, and especially Wayne Chambliss. Bob Holman of the Bowery Poetry Club and Roman Kaplan of the Russian Samovar let us use their venues for OBERIU-related performances in New York City, and we are grateful to all who took part in them.

Earlier versions of these translations have appeared in *American Poetry Review, Ars-Interpres, Boston Review, Columbia, Conjunctions, Dirigible, Emergency Gazette, Fascicle, Fence, Germ, Jubilat, New American Writing, Octopus, Open City, Poetry Project Newsletter, Rattapallax, RealPoetik, Symposion, 3rd Bed,* and *Watchword.* The editor wishes to thank the American Council of Learned Societies, the Social Science Research Council, the National Endowment for the Humanities, the MacDowell Colony, the Wytter Bynner Foundation, and the Santa Fe Art Institute for the fellowship and residencies that enabled him to focus on this volume.

Our warmest thanks goes out to our friends and families, whose love stayed with us throughout all the difficulties associated with this work. Two people whose support felt especially important to us did not live to see the project come to fruition. In the summer of 2002, we mailed several translations to Susan Sontag without really expecting her to respond to a letter received out of the blue. Yet Susan responded immediately, not only offering encouragement, but even asking how she could be of help. We remain forever in her debt for all the attention, enthusiasm, and generosity she showed us.

The editor would like to dedicate the anthology to the memory of his father, Joseph Ostashevsky, who passed away during the making of the manuscript. May this book be a memorial to him.

This anthology includes the work of three writers—Alexander Vvedensky, Daniil Kharms, and Nikolai Zabolotsky—who between 1927 and 1930 had been the main poets of OBERIU, the group that is sometimes described as Russia's last avant-garde. It also contains pieces by their close friends Nikolai Oleinikov, Leonid Lipavsky, and Yakov Druskin, who, despite never having been members of OBERIU, also contributed to that body of literature which in the West sometimes bears the academic label of "Russian absurdism."

The translators of this volume are not enthusiastic about the term "absurdism," since it operates in hindsight, emphasizing those features of the group's work that recall the literature of the absurd in postwar Europe at the expense of those features that relate it to previous developments in Russian avant-garde literature.[1] As for the term "OBERIU," we chose it for our title despite the facts that (a) only half of the writers included in the anthology had been OBERIU members, (b) OBERIU also included other persons who tend not to be categorized under that label,[2] and, finally, (c) the best work of the group postdates the dissolution of OBERIU. We opted for the term nonetheless because, despite all its imperfections, it is the one favored by Russian readers. Recently, some Russian scholars have started using the term *chinars*, which we shall explain subsequently, to argue that five of the aforementioned writers, with the exception of Zabolotsky, formed a cleanly delineated group, a private association in contrast to the public association of OBERIU.[3] Since this application of the *chinar* term is still disputed—there is no evidence of its use in the 1930s—we have kept it out of the book's title, but we do employ it in this introduction to designate the philosophical work of the circle even in the 1930s, since we know no other term that may be used.

Although the OBERIU-*chinar* corpus forms one of the most original and interesting phenomena in twentieth-century Russian literature, it began to appear in print in Russia only after the onset of perestroika. This is why, apart from Kharms's late prose, very little of the group's work has been available in English so far.[4] Consisting almost entirely of materials translated for the first time, our anthology aims to correct that lack.

Members of OBERIU and the *chinar* circle belonged to the first generation of writers to come of age after World War I and the October Revolution. A vast strip of psychological no-man's-land thus lies between them and their immediate predecessors, the futurists, with much OBERIU art lacking the utopian teleologies so characteristic of Russian modernism. At the same time, the OBERIU writers were students, directly and indirectly, of the more radical forms of the modernist project. Their main influences included the suprematist painter Kazimir Malevich and the late Velimir Khlebnikov, Russia's most original futurist poet.[5] Leningrad practitioners of sound poetry were among their early allies. They also kept in close contact with the analytic painters of the circle of Pavel Filonov.

OBERIU's founders Alexander Vvedensky and Daniil Kharms were born in December 1904 and 1905, respectively, to families of St. Petersburg intelligentsia.[6] When they met in Leningrad in 1925, they already had some measure of futurist tutelage. Vvedensky was working at sound poet Igor Terentiev's Phonological Section of the State Institute of Artistic Culture or, as abbreviated in

Russian, GINKhUK, whereas Kharms associated with another sound poet, Alexander Tufanov. These two masters of futurist sound poetry, known in Russian as *zaum*, regarded their work as an abstract, nonobjective linguistic art whose apparent meaninglessness in fact offered the poet-researcher an opportunity to study the relationship between sound and sense. For a brief period, Vvedensky and Kharms took part in Tufanov's workshop, called "The Order of *Zaum*-Practitioners DSO."[7]

To distance himself from the futurists, Vvedensky coined the neologism *chinar*, a term eventually extended to everyone in this anthology except Zabolotsky. This difficult but important term derives from the word *chin*, meaning "rank": "spiritual rank," explains Druskin.[8] In fact, *chin* appears in OBERIU poetry in such a way as recalls the nine ranks (*chiny*) of angels according to pseudo-Dionysius the Areopagite, the anonymous fifth-century Christian Neoplatonist whose apophasis, or use of language to negate itself, Vvedensky shares. Since *chin* is also etymologically linked to the archaic verb *chinit'*, meaning "to create or perform," *chinar* may be interpreted as a parallel to Sir Philip Sidney's Neoplatonic take on the Middle English "maker," or poet.[9] Vvedensky assumed the moniker "*chinar*, authority on nonsense" (*chinar', avto-ritet bessmyslitsy*), whereas Kharms started calling himself "*chinar*-observer" (*chinar'-vziral'nik*).

From the outset, the *chinars* are less interested in making up words than in destroying protocols of semantic coherence and linguistic realism. Narrative, simile, and metaphor fall by the wayside. Plans to collaborate with Russian formalist critics suggest that the *chinar* breaking and scrambling of narrative is an artistic radicalization of formalist analysis, presenting parts of narrative as autonomous with respect to the whole. The simile is denounced by Kharms to the slightly less radical poet Nikolai Zabolotsky. Zabolotsky also writes up his objections to what Vvedensky calls

"nonsense" (*bessmyslitsa*), defined by Zabolotsky as "alogical" joining of words. For Zabolotsky, alogism arises in unexpected
metaphors, but Vvedensky "materializes" such metaphors, treating
alogism as the end of poetic utterance and not as a means to convey
content more effectively.[10]

In 1926 and 1927, Kharms, Vvedensky, and Zabolotsky flirted
with several ideas for avant-garde groups, the most developed being
Radix, a theater company "experimenting in the area of nonemo-
tional and nonnarrative art." Seeking rehearsal space for their montage of Kharms and Vvedensky pieces entitled *My Momma's Got
Clocks All Over*, Radix approached Malevich, then director of
GINKhUK. Malevich said, "I'm an old troublemaker, and you're
young troublemakers. Let's see what happens." What happened was
that Radix fell apart. The remnants of the theater company, together
with their poetic associates, soon received the offer of a venue at the
Leningrad Press Club. However, since the poets were operating
under names that had the word "leftist," meaning avant-garde, in
them (Leftist Flank, Flank of Leftists, Academy of Leftist Classics),
and since in political discourse "leftist" designated Trotsky's fac-
tion, which was losing its struggle with Stalin in those very days, the
Press Club insisted on a name change. Thus OBERIU was born.[11]

The acronym OBERIU was supposed to stand for *Ob"edinenie
real'nogo iskusstva*, or Union of Real Art, but Kharms, a great
enthusiast of strange-sounding made-up words, insisted on replac-
ing a vowel. Being avant-garde, OBERIU felt compelled to make
public a manifesto, whose literary section was penned with characteristic assiduousness by Zabolotsky. Yet, besides the usual manifesto fodder about "keeping it real," Zabolotsky doesn't shed a
whole lot of light on what the term "real art" might mean.
(Although he does contrast it with his bête noire, *zaum*, the word
"OBERIU" itself sounds like the roaring of the same bête.)[12]
Apart from several other young writers, most notably Igor

Bakhterev and Konstantin Vaginov, OBERIU also included a theater section run by the Radix people and a section dedicated to nonnarrative film.

On January 24, 1928, the group put on its most elaborate event: "Three Leftist Hours" at the Leningrad Press Club. The first hour, namely, that of the poetry reading, took place beside or on top of imposing armoires left over from Igor Terentiev's staging of Gogol's *Inspector-General,* while the emcee weaved about on a tricycle. The second hour saw the performance of Kharms's play *Elizabeth Bam,* each of whose nineteen sections was realized in a different stylistic manner, with the intent that they appear autonomous. In the play's "plot," Elizabeth Bam is arrested for an undisclosed crime that eventually winds up being the murder of one of the people arresting her, who had been "slain" on stage a minute earlier in a verbal duel with her father. (It is *Elizabeth Bam* that first inspired comparisons between OBERIU and the theater of the absurd.) The last of the "Three Leftist Hours" was devoted to a montage of found footage entitled *Film Number One: The Meat-Grinder.* A long discussion followed.[13]

"Three Leftist Hours" was the most elaborate of many OBERIU events around Leningrad, in which readings alternated with circus tricks and elements of happenings. The debates they ended in sometimes got out of hand: despite the formalist critic Viktor Shklovsky's jeer that "You guys don't even know how to throw a good scandal!" the OBERIU clearly did know how to do just that.[14] On that poetry scene, scandals came with the territory. The aesthetic doctrines of the Party that began to crystallize after 1925 were not only semiliterate and wildly reactionary but also genuinely popular. Student audiences especially were full of activists who felt entitled to easy listening with a message, and when instead they got Vvedensky with his plotless compositions and deliberately monotonous reading style, they objected, and vocally.

Newspaper reviews of OBERIU shows make for reading that is both curious and ominous. The reviews are curious because they all understand OBERIU work as *zaum*, that is, as absolutely and purposefully meaningless.[15] They are ominous in that they gradually pass from strong disapproval on aesthetic grounds to vitriolic denunciation on political ones. In November 1927 the newspapers scoff at OBERIU's "ornamental spots of phonetic suprematism." By April 1930 they inveigh that the members of OBERIU "despise the struggle conducted by the proletariat. Their retreat from life, their meaningless poetry, their transrational [*zaumnoe*] juggling constitute a protest against the dictatorship of the proletariat. This is why their poetry is counterrevolutionary. It is the poetry of strangers, the poetry of class enemies."[16] This article put an end to the public activity of OBERIU.

In 1928, Nikolai Oleinikov, a poet closely associated with the OBERIU group although never officially a member, had invited Kharms, Vvedensky, and Zabolotsky to write for a children's magazine he was editing, the *Hedgehog*. Kharms in particular—despite, or perhaps because of, his dislike of real kids—found in that kind of literature a genuine second calling: his children's writing is easily among the best and most popular in the language. Yet even here the work of OBERIU members was far from uncontroversial. The campaign against "lack of message" in children's literature started in 1928, when Lenin's widow Nadezhda Krupskaia panned "The Crocodile" by Kornei Chukovsky as "incredible rubbish" that says nothing about the real life of crocodiles. Newspaper polemic erupted, and *Hedgehog* writers were promptly dragged through the mud as practitioners of similar "formalism."[17]

On December 10, 1931, Kharms, Vvedensky, the *zaum* poet Alexander Tufanov, and several others were incarcerated and, after lengthy interrogations, charged with counterrevolutionary agitation in the form of *zaum* poetry and sabotage in the field of children's literature. The interrogator viewed Kharms and Vvedensky's attempt to distract Soviet children from Socialist goals as a continuation of their brief membership in Tufanov's Order of *Zaum*-Practitioners DSO. He concluded that *zaum* was an encrypted form of communication employed for anti-Soviet propaganda; disappointingly, the dossier reveals no effort to come up with a cipher key or otherwise decode *zaum* texts.[18] Tufanov was sentenced to five years in labor camps; Kharms to three in the camps, later changed to internal exile, that is, abolition of the right to live in large cities; Vvedensky to three years of internal exile. Kharms and Vvedensky returned to Leningrad in the winter of 1933, their terms suddenly reduced. The less lucky Tufanov did time in the camps and never lived in Leningrad afterward.

The poets were allowed to again take up children's literature, but other public literary activity was out of the question. Even as members of OBERIU, their efforts to publish resulted in next to nothing; the ever-more-stifling air of the thirties made print unthinkable. Instead, they resumed activity as *chinars*, forming an unofficial circle that included Oleinikov and the philosophers Leonid Lipavsky and Yakov Druskin. Zabolotsky attended some meetings, but aesthetic, political, and personal differences made his presence progressively marginal. The dynamics of the circle showed an extraordinary level of intellectual give-and-take. More than keen critics of one another's work, the *chinars* constantly adopted and developed one another's terms and concepts. The breadth of their interests may be seen in their lively *Conversations*, written down and edited by Lipavsky. The group met regularly for several years, although by the mid-1930s it started coming apart from internal frictions.

In 1936, Vvedensky married and moved to Kharkov. In late spring 1937, the authorities, discovering political allegory in a children's poem by Kharms, blacklisted him—as it turned out, temporarily.

On July 20, Oleinikov was arrested and made to confess to membership in a counterrevolutionary Trotskyite terrorist organization at the employ of Japanese intelligence services. He was shot on November 24. March 1938 saw the detention of Zabolotsky, by then fully estranged from the group and trying his hand at Stalinist verse of unprecedented quality. Sentenced as a member of a terrorist organization of writers, he wound up spending eight years in the camps and exile.[19]

On June 22, 1941, Nazi Germany invaded the Soviet Union. Lipavsky volunteered in an antiaircraft unit and fell in the suburbs of Leningrad in November 1941. Soviet retreat was accompanied by fresh arrests of persons who had already been convicted of political crimes. Kharms, incarcerated on August 23, faced charges of agitating for defeat. The interrogator forced him to undergo a psychiatric examination. Kharms remained his usual self with the doctors and died of starvation in a prison psychiatric ward on February 2, 1942. Vvedensky, unable to push his way onto a train of evacuees in Kharkov, was detained on September 27, 1941, and accused of plotting to remain in Kharkov under German occupation. He died on December 19, 1941, on a prison train headed for Kazan, allegedly of pleurisy.[20]

With Leningrad under siege, the *chinar* Yakov Druskin retrieved a suitcase of Kharms's papers from the latter's apartment. He started sorting through it only in the 1950s, when it became clear his friends were not coming back. The suitcase held the writings of Kharms and a fraction of what had been written by Vvedensky, almost all of the rest now lost. Between 1978 and 1984, Druskin's disciple Mikhail Meilakh managed to publish Russian-language editions of Kharms and Vvedensky in West Germany and the United States, but not before being himself incarcerated for allegedly anti-Soviet literary activity.[21] Perestroika and the subsequent collapse of the Soviet Union opened the floodgates for

OBERIU publications, which, in Vvedensky's case, again slammed shut in the mid-1990s due to unscrupulous application of copyright laws.

OBERIU writers start off by regarding intuition as the tool for obtaining knowledge of things-in-themselves, that is, of the "true reality" inaccessible to perception and reason. Here OBERIU fits perfectly with Russian modernist trends. In turn-of-the-century Russia, even academic neo-Kantians resented Kant's claim that the thing-in-itself cannot be known. The philosophers found relief by appealing to intuition: not the Kantian intuitions of space and time but the Bergsonian insight bordering on sixth sense. Art, as the activity proper to such insight, was assigned the task of bridging the gap between the mental and the real. Art, argued the philosophers, is the product of perception above the senses and reason above reason; it is art that provides us with a window upon the true structure of the world.[22] This idea proved seminal for Russian modernist schools from symbolism all the way to suprematism. Rather than entertainment, however refined, Russian modernist art regarded itself as a multiform philosophical, and almost a scientific, experiment in finding superior ways of knowing. The prize here surely goes to the painter Mikhail Matiushin, for his proposal that we train ourselves to "see" with the occiput.[23]

Apart from the appeal to intuition, Russian philosophers sometimes debunked Kant with Kant's own procedure of using reason to rein in reason.[24] OBERIU thought also manifests that critical strategy, except that its critique consists of using language to rein in language. OBERIU writers referred to the language that was the object of their critique as "human language" or "human logic" or both; I will refer to it as "normative." The language that was the tool of their critique they usually called "alogist"; I will do the same. Their concept of normative language was far broader than

Kant's concept of reason: it included not only logic and a priori categories such as causality, quantity, succession, and so forth, but also grammatical and metaphoric structures as well as standard rules for classification of concepts. All of this was regarded as constituting the single system by which we (mis)cognize the world, in that our understanding mistakes cognitive relations for unknown real relations among objects and mistakes properties of language for properties of the world. Therefore, to see the world as it really is, we must first destabilize language. In the 1930s, Vvedensky looked back at his part in the project thus:

> I raised my hand against concepts, against initial generalizations that no one previously had touched. Thereby I performed, you might say, a poetic critique of reason—more fundamental than that other, abstract [critique of Kant]. I doubted that, for instance, house, cottage, and tower come together under the concept of building. Perhaps, the shoulder must be linked to the number four. I did it practically, in my poems, as a kind of proof. And I convinced myself that the old relations are false, but I don't know what the new ones must be like. I don't even know whether they should form one system or many.[25]

Vvedensky regards his poetry as an experimental inquiry into the relationship between normative language and the world. He has tested this relationship and found it wanting. Yet, as will become characteristic of the period after the dissolution of OBERIU, he no longer feels capable of fashioning a new linguistic system, one that adequately conveys reality.

Members of OBERIU described the group's poetics as "alogist," "supralogist," or even as "the poetics of meaninglessness" *(bessmyslitza)*. Apart from discrediting normative language, their alogism strove to generate such nonnormative statements as would somehow say things about the world that regular language could not. Thus, Kharms and Vvedensky read figurative speech as if it were nonfigurative (materialization of metaphor). They formed lines that are impossible either semantically or syntactically. They used rhyme as a tool for introducing absurdity into content. Yet the statements they produced, rather than being devoid of meaning, wound up making a kind of wider sense. The responsibility for this wider sense lay precisely with intuition, whose role in OBERIU work was all the greater because the usual linguistic mechanisms for constructing statements could no longer be trusted. Intuition provided the only criterion by which a given nonnormative utterance could be declared "right." Such rightness was not aesthetic but, as it were, ontological: Vvedensky used to say that one should not judge art as beautiful or not beautiful, but only as true or false.[26]

In contrast to logical reasoning, which rests on order and continuity, intuition proceeds in leaps and bounds. Alogist statements take this feature of intuition to its logical extreme. They may be discontinuous syntactically, as when Kharms writes about ripping lace "from maid from oak." They may be discontinuous semantically, as when Kharms writes about "white elephants of fear." They may be discontinuous only situationally, as when Kharms writes about the four-legged crow hobbling home on its five legs. (Situational discontinuity is the benchmark of alogism: none of these examples can be rephrased in normative language, because no "real-life" configuration of things may be found to correspond to the alogist statement.) Discontinuity manifests itself even more on the level of plot. Lipavsky and Vvedensky charge the plots of realist novels with lack of realism because psychological motivation lends them inner coherence. Excessive coherence does not seem to have plagued Vvedensky's lost novel, *Murderers, You Morons,* which even Kharms found hard to understand.[27] Kharms's short fictions string events together arbitrarily, with pointedly superficial justifications: even his late, more conventionally realist work emphasizes discontinuity in its plot structure.

Discontinuity in alogist texts aims to destroy the relations we perceive among things. Such relations can be paradigmatic—as when Vvedensky doubts that "house," "cottage," and "tower" come together under a single, more general concept of "building"—or syntagmatic, that is, those of ordering. The very principle of ordering becomes a target for attack. Kharms repeatedly rejects the most basic sequence of all, that of the natural numbers. His snipe in "The Daughter of Patruliov" that seventeen is the successor of six fits into his argument that numbers are not abstract, ordered quantities but rather qualities not subject to more or less. Impossibility of ordering renders causal relations illusory: "Real relations among objects cannot be seen in light of the causal sequence," says Lipavsky.[28] It also discredits rules of inference, opening them to violation in Kharms's parodies of logical and mathematical proofs. Even the basic categories of identity and difference are destabilized by recourses to tautology or, conversely, by inexplicable renaming of characters in the middle of the piece.

Once the relations that language lays among things break down, the world becomes a set of discrete, unconnected objects—or so it seems. For early Kharms, physical discreteness of objects reproduces itself on the ontological level: independence from relations returns the object to ontological autonomy, lets it be its full self. Kharms portrays this state, which he calls the fifth or essential meaning of the object, in Chagall-like images of flight. "The object SOARS," he writes in 1927.[29] A fabulous example of the soaring of objects may be found in his "To Ring—To Fly," where it is paralleled by violations of syntax, with the "freed" verbs falling into the infinitive.

However, the exhilarating, disjunctive, flying world of Kharms soon also falls victim to dissolution. Not just the universe as a whole, but each of its components—for example, objects—consists of a network of relations among its own, smaller parts. If you are systematic enough in getting rid of relations, the object vanishes. "Objects have disappeared," Kharms declares in 1930. He describes the mental experiment leading to the disappearance of objects as "thinking fluidly." "There are no objects," echoes Vvedensky several years later.[30] In making objects vanish, the poets take their project of destroying relations to its logical—and absurd—extreme. When, after the dissolution of OBERIU, Kharms and Vvedensky intensify their contact with Lipavsky, Druskin, and Oleinikov, forming the circle some scholars call the *chinars,* their thought embarks in a new direction. They become concerned not with absolute reality but with multiple models of reality; not with breaking of relations but with relativism and phenomenological description.[31]

Vvedensky's meditations on time in his *Gray Notebook,* which come out of his prison experience, have no place for the ontological autonomy of objects. Rather, objects are forms or, as he puts it, "feeble mirror images" of time. He is not talking about the abstract, linear time of science, however, but of the complex, shifting, subjective time that is the very fabric of our being in the world. Although such time constitutes the totality of our experience, we are not equipped to have knowledge of it: "our logic and our language skid along the surface of time." The only way we can get closer to time is to understand that we do not understand it. "Any person who has not understood time to some extent—and only someone who has not understood it, has understood it even a little bit—must cease to understand everything that exists." Either borrowing or reinventing the concepts of negative theology, Vvedensky converts incomprehension (*neponimanie*) into a directed act of unknowing that is the only epistemologically proper attitude toward being in the world.[32]

The rest of the *chinar* circle also envision time not in terms of classical physics, but as something heterogeneous, qualitative, and fragmented. Time overall resembles an environment of varying processes, or hills and gullies generating their own private times. The observer experiences time only when he notices the differences between himself and these processes, when he contrasts their transformations with his own. His noncoincidence with the (mutually noncoinciding) rhythms of the world produces the sensation of motion. Coincidence, on the other hand, or repetition, results in a momentary halt in time, which solidifies his world into a single, undifferentiated, Eleatic unity. His experience of time is thus subject to "speeding up," "slowing down," freezing, or disappearing altogether. In "Death," Druskin breaks his trips to the pharmacy down into "large moments": running to a big building was one large moment, running past the bar another, running up the stairs yet another. After one moment ends but before another begins, there gapes the infinitesimal, empty interval: the abyss harboring the petrifaction of time.

Related to the *chinar* understanding of time as a qualitative environment is their concept of the neighboring world. It intends a life formed according to other rules, as, for instance, in an environment where all distinctions are those of temperature. Yet the life of the observer and the life of his cat, or even his life and that of another observer, are also lives formed by distinct rules—and so may be looked at through the concept of neighboring worlds as well. "Neighboring" means they may occur in one place; they may consist of two ways of seeing the same place. When there are two speakers in a room, there are two neighboring worlds. On a cosmological level, the concept may be extended to that of possible worlds, and even the world of the dead: they too may be thought of as occupying the same place as ours.

An entity from one world appearing in another is called a "messenger," the literal translation of the Greek *aggelos*, which otherwise yields "angel." In the sense in which one observer's world differs from another observer's world, any communication between them takes place between messengers: one observer appears as the messenger of his own world in the world of another observer. Yet most commonly in *chinar* work a messenger is a hypothetical, extrasensory visitor from an overlapping possible world, a world whose temporality is closer to that of trees than to that of human beings.[33] In pieces on messengers in this anthology, such strong-case messengers are, to some extent, metaphors of inspiration.

Late alogism is indeed metaphorical, although the metaphors it deals with are indefinite—open-ended metaphorical structures rather than metaphors per se. The *chinars* referred to such metaphors as "hieroglyphs." The window, for example, is a hieroglyph designating the border between two neighboring worlds. The mirror, whose two-dimensional surface reflects the three-dimensional world in inverse symmetry, poses the question of how one world might reproduce another. Water is a particularly complicated hieroglyph: its surface shares the properties of the window and the mirror, while its depth, as a material environment whose regions undergo differently paced transformations, evokes the *chinar* understanding of time. Animals and trees offer examples of lives shaped by rules that are so other as to be incomprehensible. And so on.

In the 1930s, the group's critique of language also enters a new phase, one that holds language, and, in particular, nouns, responsible even for our belief in the existence of objects. Vvedensky's *Gray Notebook* emphasizes the incomprehensibility of language, in that it is not clear what aspects of reality words refer to, if any. "Language," says Lipavsky, "cuts the world into pieces." His

"Theory of Words" proposes an ur-language composed of verbs and indicating processes only. If the world really consists not of objects but of events, or, as the *chinars* call them, "waves," then neither normative nor alogist language provide anything even remotely resembling an adequate description of it.[34] The pointlessness of naming is the subject of Vvedensky's "Frother," whose plot revolves around attempts to ascertain the meaning of a made-up word, which is both the same and not the same as the meaning of (real) death, and whose definition is both already known and not known at all. If the word *frother* "stands for" the froth of death on the face of the dying father, or even for death in general, that still discloses nothing about death.

The Greek philosopher Cratylus, whom Aristotle credits with the extremely OBERIU-like correction of Heraclitus that you can't step into the same river even once, gave up on speaking—for, since an object at time *A* is not the same object at time *B*, objects have no identity and the word "dog" has no real dog to refer to. However, Cratylus still had needs and so he took his index finger and pointed. Was he right to do so? Wasn't even pointing a form of lying? It wasn't. By pointing, Cratylus asserted only that something seemed to him to be present there and then, but not that it was a dog, or even that it was something. Vvedensky's language in its late phase operates in a similar manner. The huge lyrical force of his final writings comes from his turning words into pointers, as it were: into questions rather than answers. The word "death" becomes shorthand for "What is this we call death?", the word "time" becomes shorthand for "What is this we call time?", the word "God" becomes shorthand for "What is this we call God?"[35]

We can situate the *chinars* in their social context. We can attribute the loneliness and indeterminacy pervading their writing to their isolation as writers. We can regard their critique of language as a reaction to the ever-increasing mendacity of their linguistic environment. We can read the violence, despair, and fragmentation of their late work in terms of what was happening in the apartment next door. We can become discombobulated at their jokes, cracked in expectation of arbitrary arrest. Yet how they lived and died ultimately doesn't explain how they wrote: otherwise, plenty of other people would have written the same way. This is why their work is not a historical curiosity; this is why it can speak to us, even if from a neighboring world.

Notes

For complete bibliographic information, see "Works Cited," page 255. All translations unless otherwise noted are the editor's.

1. But see Jaccard 1991, 204–81, and Tokarev 2002.

2. But see Roberts 1997.

3. Sazhin 1990.

4. Earlier translations of OBERIU in English include Kharms and Vvedensky 1997; Kharms 1993; Zabolotsky 1999; and a few pieces in Todd and Hayward 1993. For translations in Italian, French, and German, see Charms 1992; Charms 2003; Harms 1993; Vvedenski 2002; Vvedenskij 1986.

5. For Malevich and OBERIU, see Levin 1978.

6. Most of our biographical information comes from the introductions and appendices to Vvedenskii 1993 and Sazhin et al. 1998.

7. For *zaum*, see Janecek 1996.

8. Sazhin et al. 1998, 1:549.

9. "The Greekes named him ποιητήν, which name, hath as the most excellent, gone through other languages, it commeth of this word ποιεῖν which is to make: wherin I know not whether by luck or wisedome, we Englishmen have met with the Greekes in calling him a Maker." Sidney 1963, 7.

10. For plans to collaborate with the formalists on a book, see Kharms 2002, 1:287. Simile in Bakhterev 1977, 58; Zabolotsky's letter in Vvedenskii 1993, 2:174–76.

11. Meeting with Malevich in Vvedenskii 1993, 2:130–31. Due to the idiosyncratic nature of Malevich's Russian, his quip also means, "I'm an old nonfigurative artist, and you're young nonfigurative artists." Calendar of Trotsky's defeat in Conquest 1968, 12–13.

12. "The OBERIU Manifesto" in English in Kharms and Vvedensky 1997, 245–54.

13. *Elizabeth Bam* in English in Kharms and Vvedensky 1997, 155–77. Analysis in Meilakh 1991b.

14. Vvedenskii 1993, 1:23.

15. As a literary term, *zaum* refers to sound poetry only. Although OBERIU events sometimes included extemporized *zaum* speeches, one even "with a Marxist slant," Kharms was the only writer in the group to use *zaum* with any frequency, and Zabolotsky went so far as to claim in "The OBERIU Manifesto" that "no school is more inimical to us than *zaum*." However, in spoken Russian, *zaum* can be employed to brand any utterance as deliberately unintelligible. It is this popular meaning that reviewers and, later, state security applied to the literary term. For *zaum* in OBERIU, see Meilakh 1991a.

16. D. Tolmachev, "Dadaisty v Leningrade," and L. Nil'vich, "Reaktsionnoe zhonglerstvo," quoted in Vvedenskii 1993, 2:144–45, 152–54.

17. Ustinov 1990, 126.

18. Dossiers in Mal'skii 1992 and Sazhin et al. 1998, 2:519–72. An earlier interrogation of the ex-futurist Igor Terentiev "found" that *all* types of abstract art from suprematism to OBERIU were used to transmit enciphered messages about the Soviet Union to its enemies abroad (Vvedenskii 1993, 1:31). One imagines the Fifth Congress of the Enemies of the Soviet Union: "Invade now?" "Nein! Vait until Kazimir Malevitch paint green zirkle!"

19. Oleinikov's dossier in introduction to Oleinikov 2000, 40–42; Zabolotsky's memoirs of arrest in Zabolotskii 2002, 44–54; Zabolotsky's Stalinist poems in Platt 2003.

20. Kharms's dossier in Sazhin et al. 1998, 2:592–607; Vvedensky's dossier in Meilakh 1998; circumstances of Vvedensky's death in Sazhin 2004.

21. Vvedenskii 1980–84; Kharms 1978–88.

22. For neo-Kantians, see Rosenthal 1995; for Bergson, see Fink 1999.

23. Henderson 1983, 238–99.

24. See, for example, "Kosmologicheskie antinomii Immanuila Kanta," in Florenskii 1994–98, 2:3–33.

25. Sazhin et al. 1998, 1:186.

26. Ibid., 1:560.

27. Ibid., 1:183–84; 242.

28. Ibid., 1:184.

29. Levin 1978.

30. "The Eleven Assertions of Daniil Ivanovich Kharms," in Kharms and Vvedensky 1997, 117; objects in Vvedensky 2002, 12.

31. For *chinar* philosophy, see Jaccard 1991 and Iampol'skii 1998.

32. Vvedensky 2002, 9–10.

33. Sazhin et al. 1998, 1:773–74.

34. For Lipavsky on language and the "wave structure of the world," see Sazhin et al. 1998, 1:187–88; 254–320.

35. Cratylus in *Metaphysics* 1010a10–16; Druskin remembers Vvedensky saying his work had three themes: time, death, and God [Vvedenskii 1993, 2:167].

Although some OBERIU poetry is in free verse, the main body of it is in meter and rhyme. OBERIU poets often use meter and rhyme to generate lines, especially when such lines are nonsensical. One might say that rhyme for OBERIU is a more traditional version of chance operations. Yet, because in Russian and English the rhyme words almost never match and the same meters have different connotations, that aspect of OBERIU alogism defies reproduction. (Of course, even the act of rhyming in contemporary American English does not have the same connotation as in 1930s Russian.) Our versions have fewer rhymes than the originals. Our meters are often approximations. In cases when close paraphrases would be "more like" the original than word-for-word versions, we opted for paraphrase. What we really strove for was neither Russian poetry with English words nor American poetry with Russian content, but texts that tried to communicate what the strangeness and the beauty of the Russian originals feel like in American English.

As far as selection is concerned, we have decided against replicating George Gibian's translations in *The Man with the Black Coat* and Neil Cornwell's translations in Kharms's *Incidences*. However, our approach to Zabolotsky is so different from Daniel Weissbort's as to warrant the inclusion of several pieces covered in his version of Zabolotsky's *Selected Poems*.

All the translators in this book are Russian-American poets living in New York and associated with Ugly Duckling Presse, with the qualification that Thomas Epstein's membership in all of the aforementioned classes is of the honorary variety.

OBERIU

Alexander Vvedensky

Kuprianov and Natasha

Kuprianov and his dear lady Natasha after walking those swinish guests to the door prepare for bed.

KUPRIANOV [*said, taking off his majestic tie*]:
    Frightening the dark the candle burns,
    it has silver bones.
    Natasha,
    why do you stroll about yearning,
    the guests are probably for certain long since gone.
    I even forgot, Marusia,
    Sonia,
    O darling let us go to bed,
    I want to dig around in you
    in search of interesting things.
    It's not for nothing they say we have different constitutions.
NATASHA [*taking off her blouse*]:
    Kuprianov, there's little sense in this candle,
    I fear it wouldn't have lit up a poodle,
    and there's two of us here.
    I fear I will howl
    from anguish, passion, terror, thought,
    I fear you O mistress shirt,
    you that hides me within,
    I'm entangled in you like a fly.

KUPRIANOV [*taking off his jacket*]:

    Soon you and I, Natasha,
    will embark on our funny recreation.
    The two of us, the two of us
    will occupy ourselves with procreation.
    We will become like tuna.

NATASHA [*taking off her skirt*]:

    O God, I'm left without a skirt.
    What am I to do in my painted pants.

Meanwhile on chairs stood goblets, rather silver and pert,
wine blackened like a monk
and the moribund worm twitched.

    I resume.
    I feel even shame.
    I'm becoming naked like the sky,
    nothing is visible as yet,
    but soon a star will twinkle.
    It's so disgusting.

KUPRIANOV [*taking off his pants*]:

    I too will soon appear at your side
    almost naked like the tide.
    I do remember at such moments once
    I felt transported by a sacred rapture
    as I encountered a woman's fountainhead
    green or blue
    but it was red.
    I laughed like somebody who's lost his mind,
    petting the satin hemispheres of her behind.
    Yes, I was happy.

And I thought woman is a reed,
she is almost human,
an unattainable duck.
Hurry up please.

NATASHA [*taking off her pants*]:

Shedding my plumage
I think of how I'm causing stimulation
to your olfactory glands
and optic nerves.
You gorge yourself upon my earthly image
and can foretaste the pleasure
of standing upon me like a tower two o'clock.
You glimpse the hair through my shirt,
divine the beating of my wave,
but why then does my mind cloud up,
I'm half asleep like boredom.

KUPRIANOV [*taking off his lower pants*]:

I'll take these off too, I suppose,
to make me different from a corpse,
to bring our epidermises close.
Let us examine our faces in the glass:
I'm moderately mustachioed. This flush
is caused by passion.
My eyes flash and I tremble.
And you are beautiful and clear,
your breasts are like two basins,
maybe we're devils.

NATASHA [*taking off her shirt*]:

Look, I'm absolutely naked,
I have become one long face,
that's how I get in the bathtub.

Here from my sides two brown shoulders
stick out like candles,
beneath them swell two breasts,
the nipples lie on them like medals,
a belly sits below, deserted,
and also my modest furry entrance
and two extremities, significant and sparkling,
between which we are left darkling.
Perhaps you wish to see the landscape of my dark,
perhaps you wish to see the landscape of my back.
Here are two pleasant shoulder blades
like soldiers slumbering in tents
and further on the wondrous seat,
its heavenly sight
must strike you.

And the moribund worm twitched,
nothing sang
as she displayed her intricate body.

KUPRIANOV [*taking off his shirt*]:
How everything is boring
and monotonously nauseating,
look, like a naked herring
I stand before you, luxuriating,
and my fourth arm
points mightily to the skies.
If only someone came to look at us,
we are alone alone with Christ
upon this icon.
It's interesting to know how long we took to undress.
Half an hour, I reckon. What's your guess?

Meanwhile they embraced
and approached the marriage bed.
"You are definitively dear to me Natasha,"
says Kuprianov.
She lies below and lifts her legs
and tongueless the candle burns.

NATASHA:

So, Kuprianov, I am down.
Make the dark come.
The last ring of the world
that isn't yet pried apart
is you upon me.

And the black apartment
smirked momentarily above them from afar.

Lie down lie down Kuprianov,
we'll die soon.

KUPRIANOV:

No, I don't want to. [*Leaves.*]

NATASHA:

How horrible, I am alone,
I am a stone, I am a moan,
I am so sad, I am so lonely
moving my hand only. [*Cries.*]

KUPRIANOV [*indulging in solitary pleasure on a chair*]:

I entertain myself.
OK, it's over,
get dressed.

The moribund worm nods off.

NATASHA [*putting on her shirt*]:

> I took you off for the act of love
> because the world is not enough,
> because the world does not exist,
> because it's above me.
> So here I am a solitary ape
> with my insane shape.

KUPRIANOV [*putting on his shirt*]:

> Look Natasha it's getting light out.

NATASHA [*putting on her pants*]:

> Leave me alone. Get out of my sight.
> I tickle myself.
> I swell with marvelous joy.
> I am my own fountainhead.
> I love another.
> I silently put on slumber.
> From my state of nakedness
> I will pass to the conflagration of clothes.

KUPRIANOV [*putting on his lower pants*]:

> I have no hopes.
> I feel myself grow smaller,
> airless and angrier.
> The eyes of such emotional ladies
> send fires through my body's alleys.
> I'm not myself.

The moribund worm yawns.

NATASHA [*putting on her skirt*]:

> What shame, what shamelessness.
> I'm with a total bastard.

He is the ordure of humanity
and the likes of him will also become immortal.

It was night. There was nature.
The moribund worm yawns.

KUPRIANOV [*putting on his pants*]:

O natural philosophy, O logic, O mathematics, O art,
it's not my fault I believed in the force of the last emotion.
O how everything goes dark.
The world ends by choking.
I make it sick,
it makes me sick.
Dignity sinks into the final clouds.
I never believed in any quantity of stars,
I believed in one star.
It turned out I was a solitary rider
and we didn't become like tuna.

NATASHA [*putting on her blouse*]:

Look idiot look
at the extremities of my breasts.
They vanish, they retreat, they float off,
touch them you fool,
they are on the edge of a long sleep.
I turn into a larch tree,
I swell.

KUPRIANOV [*putting on his jacket*]:

I said that the female is almost human,
she is a tree.
What's there to do.
I'll smoke, I'll sit around, I'll think.

It seems stranger and stranger
that time still moves,
that it breathes.
Can time be stronger than death,
maybe we're devils.
Farewell dear Natasha larch tree.
The sun rises violent as light.
I understand nothing.

He gets smaller and smaller and disappears.
Nature indulges in solitary pleasure.

September 1931
Translated by Eugene Ostashevsky

» » »   « « «

Rug/Hydrangea

I regret that I'm not a beast,
running along a blue path,
telling myself to believe,
and my other self to wait a little,
I'll go out with myself to the forest
to examine the insignificant leaves.
I regret that I'm not a star,
running along the vaults of the sky,
in search of the perfect nest
it finds itself and earth's empty water,
no one has ever heard of a star giving out a squeak,
its purpose is to encourage the fish with its silence.
And then there's this grudge that I bear,
that I'm not a rug, nor a hydrangea.
I regret I'm not a roof,
falling apart little by little,
which the rain soaks and softens,
whose death is not sudden.
I don't like the fact that I'm mortal,
I regret that I am not perfect.
Much much better, believe me,
is a particle of day a unit of night.
I regret that I'm not an eagle,
flying over peak after peak,

to whom comes to mind
a man observing the acres.
I regret I am not an eagle,
flying over lengthy peaks,
to whom comes to mind
a man observing the acres.
You and I, wind, will sit down together
on this pebble of death.
It's a pity I'm not a grail,
I don't like that I am not pity.
I regret not being a grove,
which arms itself with leaves.
I find it hard to be with minutes,
they have completely confused me.
It really upsets me terribly
that I can be seen in reality.
And then there's this grudge that I bear,
that I'm not a rug, nor a hydrangea.
What scares me is that I move
not the way that do bugs that are beetles,
or butterflies and baby strollers
and not the way that do bugs that are spiders.
What scares me is that I move
very unlike a worm,
a worm burrows holes in the earth
making small talk with her.
Earth, where are things with you,
says the cold worm to the earth,
and the earth, governing those that have passed,
perhaps keeps silent in reply,
it knows that it's all wrong.
I find it hard to be with minutes,

they have completely confused me.
I'm frightened that I'm not the grass that is grass,
I'm frightened that I'm not a candle.
I'm frightened that I'm not the candle that is grass,
to this I have answered,
and the trees sway back and forth in an instant.
I'm frightened by the fact that when my glance
falls upon two of the same thing
I don't notice that they are different,
that each lives only once.
I'm frightened by the fact that when my glance
falls upon two of the same thing
I don't see how hard they are trying
to resemble each other.
I see the world askew
and hear the whispers of muffled lyres,
and having by their tips the letters grasped
I lift up the word wardrobe,
and now I put it in its place,
it is the thick dough of substance.
I don't like the fact that I'm mortal,
I regret that I am not perfect,
much much better, believe me,
is a particle of day a unit of night.
And then there's this grudge that I bear
that I'm not a rug, nor a hydrangea.
I'll go out with myself to the woods
for the examination of insignificant leaves,
I regret that upon these leaves
I will not see the imperceptible words,
which are called accident, which are called immortality,
which are called a kind of roots.

I regret that I'm not an eagle
flying over peak after peak,
to whom came to mind
a man observing the acres.
I'm frightened by the fact that everything becomes
    dilapidated,
and in comparison I'm not a rarity.
You and I, wind, will sit down together
on this pebble of death.
Like a candle the grass grows up all around,
and the trees sway back and forth in an instant.
I regret that I am not a seed,
I am frightened I'm not fertility.
The worm crawls along behind us all,
he carries monotony with him.
I'm scared to be an uncertainty,
I regret that I am not fire.

1934
Translated by Matvei Yankelevich

Frother

3 PARTS

The sons stood by the wall, flashing their feet shod in spurs. They rejoiced and said:

> Promulgate to us dear father
> What is this thing called Frother.

The father, flashing his eyes, replied:

> Do not confuse, my sons
> The day of the end and the knight of spring.
> Blue, terrible and grizzled is Frother.
> I am your angel. I am your father.
> I know its cruelty,
> My death is close at hand.
> Bald spots gape on my head,
> Empty patches. I am bored.
> And should my life drag on,
> Neither a falcon nor a tuft of hair
> Will remain anywhere.
> This means death is at hand.
> This means hello boredom.

The sons twinkled their bells and then rattled their tongues:

> But that wasn't our question,
> Our thoughts gestate like mansions.
> Won't you tell us dear father
> What is this thing called Frother.

> And the father exclaimed, "The prologue!
> In the prologue what matters is God.
> Go to sleep, sons.
> There are dreams: watch some."

The sons lay down to sleep. Having hid mushrooms in their pockets. Even the walls seemed obedient. Many things seemed, what of it. Actually not much seemed to us nor to them. But hark! What was that? Once more the father didn't give a direct answer. And to the sons who woke anew this is what he said, exclaiming and flashing his eyebrows:

> Let the gray-haired people
> Sing and dance.
> Let them wave their arms
> Like a man.

> On a placid, beautiful day
> You diminish in breath.
> How soon I will apprehend
> The perfection of death.

> The horses rush like waves,
> Hooves clop.
> The steeds are dashing and ablaze,
> Vanished they gallop.

But how to clasp their abatement,
And are all of us mortal?
What can you tell me, O moment
Will I understand you?

The bed stands before me
I'll softly lie,
And under the wall I'll feign to be
A flag and gladioli.

Sons, sons. My hour approaches.
I'm dying. I'm dying.
Don't ride in coaches.
The end, it comes.

In rows, flashing their feet, the sons begin to dance a quadrille.
The first son, or is it the first pair, says:

Please do tell us dear father
What is this thing called Frother.

And the second son, or is it the second pair, says:

Maybe Frother is a tether,
A teether or a head in feathers.

Then the third son, or is it the third pair:

I can't understand O father
Where is Frother? What is Frother?

The father, flashing his eyes, moans menacingly:

O, I wallow in pillows!

The first son:

> Father, I pallow in willows.
> You must not die
> Before you ply reply.

The second son, dancing like a loyal subject:

> O Frother, Frother, Frother.
> O father, father, father.

Finally the third son, dancing like a gunshot:

> Dolls and dunce caps have burned out,
> I'm a boat a boat a bout.

The sons stop dancing, because it can't all be fun and games, can it. They sit mutely and quietly by their father's expired bed. They look into his wilting eyes. They wish to repeat everything. The father is dying. He becomes fleshy like a bunch of grapes. We are terrified to look into his, so to speak, face. The sons say nothing as each of them enters his own superstitious wall.

Frother is the cold froth forming on the dead man's brow. It is the dew of death, that's what Frother is.

PART TWO

The father is flying over the writing desk. But don't think he's a spirit.

> I saw, as you'd have it, a rose,
> This tedious petal of earth.
> The flower apparently was

Thinking its last thoughts.

It caressed the neighboring mountains
With the terminal breath of its soul.
Princesses floated and stars
Above in the heavenly pall.

As my sons went away
And my horse like a wave
Stood and clacked its hoof,
The moon yellowed nearby.

O flower convinced of delight,
The godly hour is at hand.
The world comes to like the dawn
And I have gone out like a light.

The father stops speaking in verse. He takes a puff on a candle, holding it in his teeth like a flute while sinking pillowlike into the armchair.

The first son enters and says: And he hasn't even answered our question. Therefore he now turns to the pillow with a question:

Pillow pillow
Tell us rather
What is this thing called Frother.

The pillow who is also the father:

I know. I know!

The second son asks in a hurry:

Then answer,
Wherefore speak you not.

The third son, utterly incensed:

> In vain are you a widow,
> O comfortable pillow.
> Reply.

The first son:

> So answer.

The second son:

> Some fire here! Fire!

The third son:

> I am going to hang somebody, I can just feel it.

The pillow, who is also the father:

> A little patience,
> Then maybe I'll answer all your questions.
> I'd like to hear you sing.
> Then maybe I'll grow loquacious.
>
> I'm so exhausted.
> Maybe art will give me a second wind.
> Farewell, pedestal.
> I wish to hear your voices set to music.

Then the sons could not deny their father's astounded request. They huddled together like cattle and broke into a universal song:

> Big brat brother Brutus,
> A marvelous Roman.
> Everyone lies. Everyone dies.

That was the first stanza.

The second stanza:

> Sang sank skittered stole
> A lonely tightrope walker.
> That acrobat. What gall.

Third stanza:

> The stallion
> In the netherworld
> Is waiting for the clarion.

And as they sang, music resounded: wonderful, extraordinary, and all-conquering. And it seemed as if there were room left in the world for various feelings. Like a miracle the sons stood around the unsightly pillow, and awaited with meaningless hope the answer to their unenviable and savage, imposing question: What is Frother? And the pillow now fluttered, now soared into the heavens like a candle, now ran through the room like the Dnieper. Father sat over the cowwheatlike writing desk, and the sons stood against the wall like umbrellas. That's what Frother is.

PART THREE

The father sat atop a bronze steed while the sons stood at his sides. And the third son stood alternately by the horse's face and the horse's tail. As was apparent to him and to us, he felt out of place. And the horse was like a wave. No one spoke a word. They were speaking in thoughts.

Now the father sitting on the steed and stroking his darling duck exclaimed mentally, flashing his eyes:

> You're waiting to hear what the father will blather.
> Will he or won't he explain what is Frother.
> O Lord I am a disconsolate widower,
> A sinless singer.

The first son bending down picked up a five-kopeck piece from the floor. He moaned mentally and started flashing his feet:

> Papa, the end is near.
> I see a crown form above your ear.
> Your breathing is tall and austere,
> You're already a Popsicle.

The second son was just as gloomy. He bent down on the other side and picked up a lady's purse. Then he cried thoughts and started flashing his feet:

> If only I were a priest
> Or a deceased released,
> I would have visited your court,
> Almighty Lord.

And the third son, standing at the horse's tail and plucking at his mustache with his thoughts, started flashing his feet:

> Where is the key to my mind?
> Where is that ray of light,
> The sudden generosity of winter?

And as he relocated to the face of the horse that was like a
wave, he smoothed his hair with his thoughts and started flashing
his feet:

> You see no eyebrows father,
> How barren are the bloodlines of Frother.

Then the father took out of his pocket the barrel of a certain
gun and, showing it to his children, exclaimed elated and loud,
flashing his eyes:

> Look: a gun barrel!
> It's so big and unsterile!

First son:

> Where? How? Teach us—

Second son:

> Everywhere. Like finches.

Third son:

> The last fear
> After mass
> Was past
> Crumbled to dust.

The gates of heaven then flew open
And a nanny came out of the barn.
She had two legs, one after another.

And this again reminded everyone of their eternal question, namely:

What is this thing called Frother?

A horrible silence descended on everything. The sons lay strewn like candy across the night room, revolving their white grizzled occiputs and flashing their feet. Superstition overpowered them all.

The nanny had two legs, one after another.
She hung in the room mercilessly smothered.

The nanny began to put the father, who had turned small as a child's bone, to bed. She sang him a song:

Over your cradle,
Drool runs down your lips
And the moon lives.
Over the grave, over the pine,
Sleep and repine.
Better not rise.
Better pulverize.
Hey there blacksmith jacksmith,
We'll sleep in your forge.
We're all prisoners.

And as they sang, music resounded: wonderful, extraordinary, and all-conquering. And it seemed as if there were room left in the world for various feelings. Like a miracle the sons stand around the father's softly expired bed. They wish to repeat everything. We are terrified to look into his, so to speak, face. And the pillow now fluttered, now soared into the heavens like a candle, now ran through the room like the Dnieper. Frother is the cold froth forming on the dead man's brow. It is the dew of death, that's what Frother is.

Dear God, the sons could have said if only they could. But we knew that already.

1936–37
Translated by Thomas Epstein, Eugene Ostashevsky,
and Genya Turovskaya

A Certain Quantity
of Conversations, or The
Completely Altered Nightbook

I. A CONVERSATION ABOUT
AN INSANE ASYLUM

Three companions were traveling by carriage. They were exchanging thoughts.

FIRST: I know the insane asylum. I saw the insane asylum.

SECOND: What are you saying? I know nothing. How it looks.

THIRD: Does it look? Who saw the insane asylum.

FIRST: What's in it? Who lives in it.

SECOND: Birds don't live in it. Time passes in it.

THIRD: I know the insane asylum, the insane live there.

FIRST: That makes me happy. That makes me very happy. Hello insane asylum.

THE MASTER OF THE INSANE ASYLUM [*looks into his decrepit little window as if it were a mirror*]: Hello friends. Please lie down.

The carriage stops at the gates. Trifles stare out from behind the fence. The evening passes. Nothing changes. Consider the poverty of language. Consider impoverished thoughts.

FIRST: So that's what it's like, the insane asylum. Hello insane asylum.

SECOND: I knew that's how it was. Just like that.

THIRD: I didn't know. Is it just like that.

FIRST: Let's go for a walk. They are walking everywhere.

SECOND: There are no birds here. Are there birds here.

THIRD: Not many of us remain and we won't remain for long.

FIRST: Write cleanly. Write boringly. Write aboundingly. Write resoundingly.

SECOND: Good, that's what we'll do.

A door opens. A doctor enters, accompanied by assistants. Everyone trembles with cold. Consider the conditions of place. Consider what happens. But nothing happens. Consider the poverty of language. Consider impoverished thoughts.

FIRST [*speaking in Russian verse*]:

> Please enter the insane asylum,
> My friends, my ends.
> It gladly awaits us.
> We gladly await us.
> We light a street lamp here,
> The light hangs like a king.
> Foxes run around here
> They piercingly squeak.
> All is temporary here
> The flowers around us creak.

SECOND: I heard these verses through. They ended long ago.

THREE: Not many of us remain and we won't remain for long.

THE MASTER OF THE INSANE ASYLUM [*opening his decrepit little window as if it were a part of the window*]: Come in, friends, lie down.

Three companions were traveling by carriage. They were exchanging thoughts.

2. A CONVERSATION ABOUT
THE ABSENCE OF POETRY

Twelve persons sat in a room. Twenty persons sat in a room. Forty persons sat in a room. Music played in the concert hall. The singer sang:

> O you poets is it true
> All your songs have been sung through.
> And the singers lie in graves,
> Just like misers they are grave.

The singer paused. A couch appeared. The singer continued:

> A tree doesn't make a sound,
> The night without honor flows.
> Quietly the sun like science
> Bakes the tedious groves.

The singer paused. The couch disappeared. The singer continued:

> Clouds roll about, bored,
> Horses gallop on a lark,
> But no poems can be heard,
> All is noiseless all is dark.

The singer paused. A couch appeared. The singer continued:

> Probably the poets died,
> The musicians and the singers.
> Probably their bodies lie
> Sleeping gravely like misers.

The singer paused. The couch disappeared. The singer continued:

O gaze upon nature

Here everybody approached the window and looked out on the paltry sight.

At the soundless forests.

Everybody gazed at the forests, which gave off not a single sound.

People now are sick and tired
Of the warbling of birds.

People stand around everywhere, spitting in disgust as birds warble.

The singer paused. A couch appeared. The singer continued:

Turning crimson, the leaf falls.
The singers' cemetery palls.
Autumn. Darkness. Nightly chill
Settles on the speechless hill.

The singer paused. The couch disappeared. The singer continued:

The sleeping poets stood upright
And said, You're exactly right.
We lie in coffins, sung to rest,
Under the pall of yellow grass.

The singer paused. A couch appeared. The singer continued:

Music plays inside the ground,
Worms with verses sing along,

Rhymes throughout rivers resound,
Beasts drink the sounds of songs.

The singer paused. The couch disappeared. The singer died. What did he prove by that.

3. A CONVERSATION ABOUT REMEMBERING EVENTS

FIRST: Let us recall the beginning of our argument. I said that I was at your place last night while you said that I wasn't. To prove my point I said that I spoke with you yesterday; but you, to prove your point, said that I didn't speak with you yesterday.

Both of them were majestically stroking their cats. Outside it was evening. A candle burned on the windowsill. Music was playing.

FIRST: Then I said: Come on, you were sitting there, at place *A*, while I stood there, at place *B*. Then you said: No, come on, you were not sitting there, at place *A*, and I was not standing there, at place *B*. To buttress my proof, to make it very very powerful, I immediately experienced sadness, joy, and lament, and then I said: But there were two of us here yesterday, at the same time, at two neighboring points, *A* and *B*—don't you understand that.

They both sat locked in a room. A sleigh rode.

FIRST: But you too washed yourself over with the emotions of indignation, ferocity, and love of truth, and you answered: You were you, I was me. You didn't see me, I didn't see you. As far as those rotten points *A* and *B* go, I don't even want to talk about them.

Two persons sat in a room. They were conversing.

FIRST: Then I said: (I remember) a groom walked on the cupboard, whistling; and (I remember) a mighty forest of flowers shook its wonderful crowns on that chest of drawers; and (I remember) a fountain babbled under the chair, and a vast palace rose under the bed. That's what I said to you. Then you smiled and answered: I remember the groom, the mighty forest of flowers, the babbling fountain, and the vast palace; but where are they, they're nowhere to be seen. We were almost certain about everything else. But it wasn't like that at all.

Two persons sat in a room. They were remembering. They were conversing.

SECOND: Then we were at the middle of our argument. You said: But you can picture me at your place yesterday. And I said: I don't know. Maybe I can picture it, but you weren't there. Then your face temporarily altered completely and you said: How can that be? How can that be? I can picture it. I won't insist any longer that I was there but I can picture it. I see it clearly: I am entering your room and I see you—you're sitting here and there, and all around hang my witnesses, the paintings and the statues and the music.

Two persons sat in a locked room. A candle burned on the table.

SECOND: You recounted all that very very persuasively, I answered; but then I briefly forgot you exist, and the witnesses are mute. Maybe that's why I can't picture anything. In fact I even doubt the existence of these witnesses. Then you said that you were beginning to experience the death of your emotions but that nonetheless, nonetheless (and weakly now), nonetheless it seemed to you that you had been at my place. I too fell silent and then said that nonetheless it seemed to me as though you hadn't. But it wasn't like that at all.

Three persons sat locked in a room. Outside it was evening. Music was playing. A candle burned.

THIRD: Let us recall the end of your argument. Neither of you said anything. That's the way it was. Truth strolled arm in arm with you like numeration. What was probable? The argument ended. I stood astounded.

Both of them were majestically stroking their cats. Outside it was evening. A candle burned on the windowsill. Music was playing. The door stayed tightly shut.

4. A CONVERSATION ABOUT CARDS

Well, let's play cards, *shouted the* FIRST.

It was early morning. It was very early morning. It was four o'clock in the morning. Not all who could have been there were there; those who were not there lay at home, wracked in their beds by terrible illnesses, while their crushed families encircled them, lamenting and pressing to their eyes. They were human. They were mortal. What can be done about it. If we look around, the same is in store for us.

Let's play cards, *that night nonetheless shouted the* SECOND.
I like playing cards, *said* SANDONETSKY, *or the* THIRD.
Cards cheer my soul, *said the* FIRST.
But where are our the one who was a woman and the one who was a girl? *asked the* SECOND.

Oh don't ask, they're dying, *said the* THIRD, *or* SANDONETSKY. Why don't we play cards.

Cards are a good thing, *said the* FIRST.

I love playing cards very much, *said the* SECOND.

They excite me. When I play I'm no longer myself, *said* SANDONETSKY. *He is also the* THIRD.

Yeah, you won't be playing cards when you're dead, *said the* FIRST. So let's play cards right now.

Why the gloomy thoughts, *said the* SECOND. I love to play cards.

And I too am cheerful, *said the* THIRD. And I love cards.

And I, how much do I love cards, *said the* FIRST. I am ready to play all the time.

You can play on the table. You can also play on the floor, *said the* SECOND. So here's what I am suggesting—let's play cards.

I'd even play on the ceiling, *said* SANDONETSKY.

I'd even play on top of a drinking glass, *said the* FIRST.

I'd even play under the bed, *said the* SECOND.

Then you start, *said the* THIRD. You start. Draw. Show me your cards. Let's play cards.

I'm ready, *said the* FIRST. I've played before.

All right, *said the* SECOND. I got nothing on my mind now. I'm a player.

I'll say without bragging, *said* SANDONETSKY. Who am I to love. I'm a player.

Well, *said the* FIRST, the players have gathered. Let's play cards.

As far as I can tell, *said the* SECOND, you've invited me and the rest of us to play cards. My answer is: I agree.

It seems that I've been invited as well, *said the* THIRD. My answer: I agree.

In my opinion the invitation also applies to me, *said the* FIRST. My answer: I agree.

I can see, *said the* SECOND, that we're all just about insane. So let's play cards. What's the use of sitting around.

Yes, *said* SANDONETSKY, as for me: I'm insane. Without cards I'm nowhere.

Yes, *said the* FIRST, if you please: it's the same with me. Wherever there are cards, there I am.

I go crazy from cards, *said the* SECOND. Play or be played.

Look, we've wrapped the night around our little finger, *said the* THIRD. Look, the night is over. Let's go home.

Yes, *said the* FIRST. It's been proven by science.

Of course, *said the* SECOND. Proven by science.

No doubt about it, *said the* THIRD. Proven by science.

They all broke into laughter and then headed for their nearby homes.

5 · A CONVERSATION ABOUT RUNNING IN A ROOM

Three persons were running around a room. They were conversing. They were moving.

FIRST: The room is not running away anywhere. I am running.

SECOND: Around the statues, around the statues, around the statues.

THIRD: There are no statues here. Look, there are no statues.

FIRST: Look: no statues here.

SECOND: Our consolation is that we have souls. Look, I'm running.

THIRD: The chair is a runaway, the table is a runaway, the wall is a runaway.

FIRST: I believe you are wrong. In my opinion we alone are running away.

Three persons sat in a garden. They were conversing. Birds loomed in the air above them. Three persons sat in a green garden.

SECOND:

When sitting in a garden
Wish upon a star,
Count how many of us
Will die before winter,

Hear the knocking of the birds,
The sound of human faces,
The roaring of beasts,
Then stand and run the farewell races.

Three persons stood on a mountaintop. They were speaking in verse. There was neither time nor place for intense movements.

THIRD:

On a mountain of late
I thought about tectonic plates.
The earth is wrinkled, black, and craggy
But terrifying is its empery.
Here's the air. Gray is its hair.
Hello air my neighbor.
I embrace this height.
God is within my sight.

Three persons stood on the seashore. They were conversing. The waves listened to them from far away.

FIRST:

I stood for long by the sea

And thought about its deep.
I thought why does it sound
Like the musician Debussy.
I knew then the sea is a garden.
With its musical swells it seems
To summon me and you
To run around the room with dreams.

Three persons were running around the room. They were conversing.
They were moving. They were looking around.

SECOND: Here everything is as before. Not a thing ran away.

THIRD: We alone are running away. Now I will take out my weapon.
I will perform an act upon myself.

FIRST: How funny. Will you shoot yourself or drown yourself or
hang yourself?

SECOND: Oh do not laugh! I am running so that I may run out faster.

THIRD: What an eccentric. He's running around statues.

FIRST: If you call all objects statues, then OK.

SECOND: I would have called stars and immobile clouds statues. As
for me, I would have.

THIRD: I am running to God. I am a runaway.

SECOND: I know that I killed myself.

Three persons left the room and rose to the roof. Why would they do
that, you'd think.

6. A CONVERSATION ABOUT
UNINTERRUPTED CONTINUATION

Three persons sat on the roof with arms folded in total tranquillity.
Sparrows flew above them.

FIRST: Now do you see, I'm taking a rope. It's strong. It's already soaped.

SECOND: What's there to speak of. I'm taking out a gun. It's already soaped.

THIRD: And there's the river. There's the ice hole. It's already soaped.

FIRST: Everyone can see I am ready to carry out my plan.

SECOND: Farewell my children, my wives, my mothers, my fathers, my oceans, my air.

THIRD: Cruel water, what am I to whisper in your ear. I think it can only be one thing: we shall soon meet.

They sat on the roof in total tranquillity. Sparrows flew above them.

FIRST: I am approaching the wall and picking a spot. Here, here's where we'll hammer in the hook.

SECOND:
As the gun barrel caught sight of me,
Death at once invited me.

THIRD: You're tired of waiting for me, congealed river. A little longer and I'll approach.

FIRST: Air, give me your hand so I can shake it in farewell.

SECOND: A little more time will pass and I'll turn into a refrigerator.

THIRD: As for me, I'll turn into a submarine.

They sat on the roof in total tranquillity. Sparrows flew above them.

FIRST: I am standing on a stool, lonely as a candle.

SECOND: I am sitting in a chair. There's a gun in my insane hand.

THIRD: Trees, the ones that stand covered in snow, and trees, the ones that stand in feathers of leaves, they stand far from this blue ice hole; I stand in a fur coat and hat as Pushkin once stood, and I that stand before this ice hole, before this water—I am an expiring man.

FIRST: I know all of that. I am throwing the rope around my own neck.

SECOND: Yes, it's all clear. I am inserting the gun barrel in my mouth. My teeth do not chatter.

THIRD: I am taking a few steps back. I am taking a running start. I am running.

They sat on the roof in total tranquillity. Sparrows flew above them.

FIRST: I am jumping off the stool. The rope is around my neck.

SECOND: I am pressing the trigger. The bullet is in the barrel.

THIRD: I have jumped into the water. There is water inside me.

FIRST: The noose tightens. I am suffocating.

SECOND: The bullet hit me. I have lost it all.

THIRD: The water filled me. I am choking.

They sat on the roof in total tranquillity. Sparrows flew above them.

FIRST: I died.

SECOND: Died.

THIRD: Died.

FIRST: Died.

SECOND: Died.

THIRD: Died.

They sat on the roof in total tranquillity. Sparrows flew above them.

They sat on the roof in total tranquillity. Sparrows flew above them.

They sat on the roof in total tranquillity. Sparrows flew above them.

7. A CONVERSATION ABOUT
VARIOUS ACTIONS

An explanatory thought. *It would seem what is there to continue when everyone died, what is there to continue. That much is clear. But do not forget, it is not three men that are acting here. It is not they that are riding in a carriage, it is not they that are arguing, it is not they that are sitting on the roof. Perhaps it is three lions, three tapirs, three storks, three letters, three numbers. What is their death to us, what is their death to them.*

Nevertheless, the three of them were sailing in a boat, exchanging oars with every minute, with every second, with such speed, with such breadth that their amazing arms were invisible.

FIRST: He blew.
SECOND: He spat.
THIRD: It all went out.
FIRST: Light.
SECOND: The candle.
THIRD: Again.
FIRST: It does not work.
SECOND: The candle again.
THIRD: Goes out.

They began to fight, beating each other about the head with hammers.

FIRST: If we only had.
SECOND: Matches.
THIRD: They would have helped.
FIRST: Not really.

SECOND: It went out.
THIRD: Too much here.

They drink acid, resting on oars. But it is really opaque all around.

FIRST: So light it.
SECOND: Light, light it.
THIRD: It's just like in Paris.
FIRST: You thought it was China.
SECOND: Are we really sailing.
THIRD: To faraway Lethe.
FIRST: Without gold or copper.
SECOND: Will we reach it by summer.
THREE: Clip.
FIRST: Skip.
SECOND: Dip.
THIRD: If dead, then.
FIRST: Not for [. . .]
SECOND: If mortal, then.
THIRD: Don't even look.

Thus they sailed in a boat, exchanging thoughts while oars flickered in their hands like gunshots.

8. A CONVERSATION BETWEEN MERCHANTS AND THE BATH ATTENDANT

TWO MERCHANTS *were wandering around a pool that had no water in it. But the* BATH ATTENDANT *was sitting under the ceiling.*

TWO MERCHANTS [*lowering their heads like oxen*]: There's no water in the pool. I'm in no condition to bathe.

BATH ATTENDANT:

> Monotonous is my routine:
> I sit up here like an owl
> As sauna steam
> And beefy air
> Writhe above each cauldron.
> I shall become
> The prey of dark,
> The child of the chaldron.
> The ovens glimmer,
> Candles fade,
> As mercilessly steam is made.
> Among damp bunks
> Shoulders shine yellow
> And boils the future
> Slaughter's tallow.
> They seek for birch,
> [. . .] money
> Here hunters become meaner.
> Within the dark
> Scour howl bark
> The father the horseman the swimmer.
> And the smoke quivers like a beggar
> Inside this dark and godless place
> Where every scoundrel's glistening face
> Loses its deathly swagger.

TWO MERCHANTS [*raising their heads as if struck dumb*]: Let's go to the women's section. I'm in no condition to bathe here.

BATH ATTENDANT [*sitting under the ceiling like a female bath attendant*]:

> When goddesses
> Make their entrance

The sky congeals
In the distance.
They throw their furs down like wings,
They bare their skirts and other things
And turning naked in an instant
From their necks they dangle infants.
Soap dances wildly like Hope,
Sponge plunges down a slippery slope.
And her eyes' bright snow,
And her speeches' flow,
And the contour of nights
And the ovens' lights
Are more frightening
Than candles' needy glow.
Here I sit among iniquity
Of multitudinous liquidity
That gushes from the open faucets
And rushes down the bodies' rapids,
Where bellies swell, recalling tyrants,
I may be a bath attendant but even I am sweating.
We female bath attendants now
Are weary and devoid of hope.
How happily that hook's screwed in.
I have a weapon. I have rope.
Let the naked ladies play,
I don't like them anyway.

TWO MERCHANTS [*staring straight into the bath like into waves*]: This attendant must be sexless.

ELIZAVETA *enters. She undresses with the clear intention of washing. The* TWO MERCHANTS *stare at her like shades.*

TWO MERCHANTS: Look. Look. She is wingèd.

TWO MERCHANTS: Yes, she's got thousands of little wings.

ELIZAVETA *does not notice the merchants. She washes, dresses, and leaves the bath.* OLGA *enters. She undresses, apparently intending to bathe. The* TWO MERCHANTS *stare at her as if into a mirror.*

TWO MERCHANTS: Look, look how I've changed.

TWO MERCHANTS: Yes, yes. I am completely unrecognizable.

Noticing the merchants, OLGA *covers her nakedness with her fingers.*

OLGA: Merchants aren't you ashamed to be looking at me.

TWO MERCHANTS: We want to bathe. And there's no water in the men's section.

OLGA: What are you thinking now.

TWO MERCHANTS: We thought you were a mirror. We made a mistake. We beg your pardon.

OLGA: Merchants I am a woman. I am modest. I cannot stand in front of you naked.

TWO MERCHANTS: How strangely you're built. You almost don't look like us. Your chest isn't the same and there's an essential difference between your legs.

OLGA: You speak strangely, merchants, can it be you have not seen our beautiful women. Merchants I am very beautiful.

TWO MERCHANTS: Olga you are bathing.

OLGA: I am bathing.

TWO MERCHANTS: So bathe, bathe.

OLGA *finished bathing. She got dressed and left the bath.* ZOIA *enters. She undresses, which means she wants to wash. The* TWO MERCHANTS *are swimming and wandering about the pool.*

ZOIA: Merchants, are you men?

TWO MERCHANTS: We are men. We are bathing.

ZOIA: Merchants, where are we. What game are we playing?

TWO MERCHANTS: We are in a bath. We are having a wash.

ZOIA: Merchants, I am going to swim around and wash. I am going to play the flute.

TWO MERCHANTS: Then swim. Wash. Play.

ZOIA: Maybe this is hell.

ZOIA finished bathing, swimming, playing. She got dressed and left the bath. The BATH ATTENDANT, who is also the female bath attendant, comes down from the ceiling.

BATH ATTENDANT: Merchants, you have made a fool of me.

TWO MERCHANTS: How?

BATH ATTENDANT: By coming in fool's caps.

TWO MERCHANTS: But what does that matter. We did not do it on purpose.

BATH ATTENDANT: It turns out that you are predators.

TWO MERCHANTS: What kind?

BATH ATTENDANT: Lions or tapirs or storks. Or maybe even hawks.

TWO MERCHANTS: Bath attendant you are shrewd.

BATH ATTENDANT: I am shrewd.

TWO MERCHANTS: Bath attendant you are shrewd.

BATH ATTENDANT: I am shrewd.

9. THE PENULTIMATE CONVERSATION, ENTITLED: ONE MAN AND WAR

A bleak situation. A military situation. A tactical situation. Almost an attack or a battle.

FIRST: I am one man and the earth.

SECOND: I am one man and the cliff.

THIRD: I am one man and war. Here's what else I have to say: I composed a poem about the year nineteen fourteen.

FIRST: I read it with no introduction of any kind.

SECOND:

> The Germans pillage the Russian land.
> I lie
> In cabbage
> Unable to understand.
> Shame on the Germans, shame on Kant.
> Every gallant
> Grenadier will avenge us.
> Grand Duke K. R.
> Plays God's sycophant.
> Observing from afar
> The Germans' actions,
> I germinated
> Like a star.
> In sight of lawyers and lawmakers
> I was tossed
> From my nest
> On my breast.

THIRD: Take a break. We need to think about this.

FIRST: Let's sit on a rock. Let's listen to gunshots.

SECOND: Everywhere, everywhere verses shed leaves like trees.

THIRD: I continue.

FIRST:

> What is it
> What happened
> I cannot accept
> The Tsaritsa was praying

To gillyflowers
To garlands
To crosses
On graves
As she tore from herself the leaves
Of innumerable infirm Russians.

SECOND: Have we really reached the communal graveyard.

THIRD: And here their remains are interred.

FIRST: Shots resound. Cannons make noise.

SECOND: I continue.

THIRD:

Battling in sore
Battles
Not yet forgotten,
I saw
Representations
Of the unfortunate
Corpses of the dead.
Up till then
They were eating pudding.
From then on
Bombardments became their bedding.
But rattling
The sword
The bird
Glittering
The bloody shirt
The corpses
In copses
Like clouds
The legs ran around like horses.

FIRST: An accurate description.

SECOND: Hear out the song or the speech of gunshots.

THIRD: You've made it all completely clear.

FIRST: I continue.

SECOND:

> How beautiful you are O war,
> I love the cheek of wine,
> The eyes and lips of wine
> And the white teeth of vodka.
> For three whole years there was shelling,
> Pillage, bombardment, and yelling.
> Bayonets, flowers, guns firing,
> Bombardment, pillage, expiring.

THIRD: Yes that's true, there was a war on back then.

FIRST: That year the hussars were beautifully dressed.

SECOND: No, the uhlans were better.

THIRD: The grenadiers were beautifully dressed.

FIRST: No, the dragoons were better.

SECOND: From that year not even the pits have remained.

THIRD: The gunshots wake. They are yawning.

FIRST [*looking out of a window shaped like the letter* A]: Nowhere do I see any writing that is connected to any concept whatsoever.

SECOND: What's surprising about that. What are we, schoolteachers.

THIRD: The merchants are passing by. Shouldn't we ask them something.

FIRST: Ask. Ask.

SECOND: Two merchants, where are you coming from.

THIRD: I was mistaken. The merchants are not passing by. They are nowhere to be seen.

FIRST: I continue.

SECOND: Why does the end come when we don't want it to.

The situation was bleak. It was military. It resembled a battle.

10. THE LAST CONVERSATION

FIRST: I left home and walked on.

SECOND: Clearly, I was walking along a road.

THIRD: The road, the road was planted all around.

FIRST: It was planted all around with oak trees.

SECOND: The trees, they made noise with their leaves.

THIRD: I sat beneath the leaves and I thought.

FIRST: I thought about that.

SECOND: About my arguably stable existence.

THIRD: I could not understand anything.

FIRST: So I stood up and again walked on.

SECOND: Clearly, I was walking along a path.

THIRD: The path, the path was planted all around.

FIRST: It was planted all around with tormentor flowers.

SECOND: The flowers, they talked in their flower language.

THIRD: I sat near them and I thought.

FIRST: I thought about that.

SECOND: About representations of death, about its eccentricities.

THIRD: I could not understand anything.

FIRST: So I stood up and again walked on.

SECOND: Clearly, I was walking on air.

THIRD: The air, the air was surrounded.

FIRST: It was surrounded by clouds and objects and birds.

SECOND: The birds, they were busy with music, the clouds fluttered about, the objects were standing in place like elephants.

THIRD: I sat nearby and I thought.

FIRST: I thought about that.

SECOND: About the feeling of life dwelling within me.

THIRD: I could not understand anything.

FIRST: So I stood up and again walked on.

SECOND: Clearly, I was walking in thought.

THIRD: The thoughts, the thoughts, they were surrounded.

FIRST: They were surrounded by illumination and sounds.

SECOND: The sounds were audible, the illumination blazed.

THIRD: I sat beneath the sky and I thought.

FIRST: I thought about that.

SECOND: About the carriage, about the bath attendant, about poems, and about actions.

THIRD: I could not understand anything.

FIRST: So I stood up and again walked on.

THE END

1936–37
Translated by Thomas Epstein and Eugene Ostashevsky

Elegy

So I composed an elegy
about a horse-and-carriage ride.

Examining the tops of mountains,
their uncountable feet,
wine-swollen vessels,
the world, like snow, in splendor,
I saw cold streams,
the storm's eyebeams,
the wind high and serene
and death's pointless hour.

> Here a knight, swimming like a cod,
> with solemn courage in his heart,
> against the agitated sea
> fights an unequal battle.
> Here a horse into mighty palms
> lays the fire of alarms
> and twilight horses do a dance
> in the hand of the stately thistle.

Where the forest looks into the fields,
into the night's silent decor,
and we look through the naked window
at the light of a soulless star,

dress our hearts in empty doubt,
wake languish whimper in the night,
we mean almost nothing,
we await an obedient life.

> We are estranged from admiration,
> we feel only perturbation,
> we cowardly betray a friend,
> the Lord is not our lord.
> We cultivated the flower of grief,
> ourselves to ourselves forgave,
> we who like ashes have grown cold
> prefer carnation to an eagle.

I look at animals with envy,
trusting in neither thoughts nor words,
our minds have suffered a loss,
there is no cause for struggle.
We apprehend all as a fall,
even the day the dream the shadow,
and even the buzz of music
won't escape the abyss.

> Neither the anxiety of the surf,
> nor deserted, discordant sand,
> nor the obscene bodies of women
> sated our yearning.
> We forgot the pose of careless calm,
> sang death, sang dearth, sang lies, sang harm,
> equated memory with hubris,
> that's why we're burning.

Divine birds fly,
their fine braids flap,

their bathrobes glint like knives,
their flight lacks mercy.
They measure off units of time,
they weigh the burden of rhyme—
ignore the empty stirrup's chime,
don't plead insanity.

> Allow the crystal stream to roam,
> the mirror horse to take it on home,
> breathing in the musical air
> you breathe in rot.
> Driver irritable and ill,
> at the last hour of sleepy dawn
> rush rush the lazy carriage
> with all you got.

No swans above the festive boards
flex the white muscles of their wings,
in tandem with bronze eagles
trumpeting hoarsely.
Eradicated inspiration
now comes for almost no duration,
orient yourself by death by death,
singer and poor horseman.

1940
Translated by Eugene Ostashevsky

»»» «« «

Where. When.

WHERE

Where he stood leaning on a statue. With his face full of thoughts.
He stood. He was turning into a statue himself. He had no blood.
Behold what he said:

> Good-bye dark trees,
> good-bye black woods,
> circumambulation of the stars
> voices of carefree birds.

He probably got it into his head to leave sometime for somewhere.

> Good-bye cliffs of the field,
> I observed you for hours.
> Good-bye living butterflies,
> I starved with you and yours.
> Good-bye rocks, good-bye clouds,
> I loved you and I made you cry out loud.

With pain and belated repentance he started examining the
ends of the grass.

> Good-bye excellent ends.
> Good-bye flower. Good-bye water.

55

The postal couriers run,
fate runs, misfortune runs.
I walked a prisoner in the field,
I embraced a path in the forest,
I awoke fish in the morning,
I frightened away a crowd of oaks,
saw the sepulchral house of oaks,
led the song around with difficulty.

He imagines and remembers how he once or never used to come out onto the shore of the river.

I used to come to you, river.
Good-bye river. My hand is shaking.
You glistened entire and flowed
and I stood before you,
dressed in a coat of glass,
and listened to your fluvial surf.
How sweet it was for me to enter
you and to come out again.
How sweet it was for me to enter
me and to come out again,
where the oaks made noise like finches
mad oaks could
hardly make noise oaks.

But here he mentally estimates what would have happened if he had also seen the sea.

Good-bye sea. Good-bye sand.
O mountain regions how high up you are.
Let the waves pound, the foam froth,

I sit on a stone with a flute
and the sea plashes gradually.
Everything is far away in the sea.
Everything is far away from the sea.
Like a boring joke, anxiety flees.
It's hard to say, Good-bye O sea.
Good-bye O sea. Good-bye paradise.
How high up you are, O mountain regions.

He also remembered the last of nature. He remembered the desert.

You too good-bye
sand lions sky.

And having thus taken leave of everything he lay down his weapon and extracting his temple out of his pocket shot himself in the head. And now part two happened—the leave-taking of everyone from the one.

The trees tossed their hands in the air like wings. They thought it over as best they could and they said:

You came to us. Behold,
he died. So shall you all.
He mistook us for minutes.
He was threadbare, rumpled, and bent,
madly wandering hither and thither
like icy winter.

What is he communicating to the trees now.—Nothing.—He is busy becoming turgid.

The cliffs or the rocks did not move. Through silence and soundlessness and saying nothing, they intimated to us and to you and to him.

> Sleep. Good-bye. The end has come.
> For you the courier has come.
> It has come the final hour.
> Lord have mercy on us.
> Lord have mercy on us.
> Lord have mercy on us.

What is he objecting to the rocks now.—Nothing.—He is busy becoming frigid.

The fish and the oaks presented him with a bunch of grapes and a modest quantity of final joy.

> The oaks said: We grow.
> The fish said: We row.
> The oaks said: What time is it with us and you.
> The fish said: Have mercy on us too.

What will he say to the fish and the oaks.—Nothing.—He won't even know how to thank them.

River imperiously running along the face of the earth. River imperiously flowing. River imperiously bearing its waves. River like a czar. It was saying good-bye in such a way that. Like that. And he lay on its very shore like a notebook.

> Good-bye notebook.
> Dying is difficult and unpleasant.
> Good-bye world. Good-bye paradise.
> You are so far away, O human regions.

What will he do to the river?—Nothing.—He is busy becoming rigid.

And the sea, worn out by long-lasting tempests, looked at death with regret. Did the sea bear a weak resemblance to an eagle.—No it did not.

Will he look at the sea?—No he cannot.

But hark! suddenly someone trumpeted, either savages or not savages. He looked at humanity.

WHEN

When he half-opened his swollen eyes, he half-opened his eyes. He recalled everything exactly as it is by heart. I forgot to say good-bye to the rest, that is, I forgot to say good-bye to the rest. Here he remembered, he recalled the entire instant of his death. All those sixes and fives. All that—running around. That rhyme. Which had been his faithful friend, as Pushkin said before him. Ah Pushkin, Pushkin, the very Pushkin who had lived before him. Here the shadow of universal repugnance lay upon everything. Here the shadow of universal lay upon everything. Here the shadow lay upon everything. He did not understand anything but he refrained from. And the savages or maybe not savages, with a weeping that resembled the rustle of oaks, the buzz of bees, the plash of waves, the silence of rocks, the view of the desert, came out holding plates over their heads and descended, without hurry, from the mountaintops onto the nonnumerous earth. Ah Pushkin, Pushkin.

THE END

1941
Translated by Thomas Epstein and Eugene Ostashevsky

Daniil Kharms

The Story of Sdygr Appr

ANDREI SEMIONOVICH: Hello, Petia.

PETR PAVLOVICH: Hello, hello. Guten Morgen. Where you going?

Andrei Semionovich stretched his hand out to Petr Pavlovich. Petr Pavlovich grabbed Andrei Semionovich's hand and jerked it so that Andrei Semionovich was left without an arm and ran off in fright. Petr Pavlovich ran after Andrei Semionovich shouting: "I tore off your arm, you scoundrel, but I'll catch up to you and, just you wait, I'll tear your head off, too!"

Andrei Semionovich took a surprising leap and cleared a ditch. Petr Pavlovich, on the other hand, were unable to jump over the ditch and were left standing on this side of it.

ANDREI SEMIONOVICH: What? You couldn't catch up to me?

PETR PAVLOVICH: Have you seen this? (And He held up the arm of Andrei Semionovich for Andrei Semionovich to see.)

ANDREI SEMIONOVICH: That's my arm!

PETR PAVLOVICH: Yes, sir, it's your arm! What will you wave with then?

ANDREI SEMIONOVICH: A handkerchief.

PETR PAVLOVICH: Not bad, not bad. What can I say? Stick one hand in a pocket and there's nothing left to scratch your head with.

ANDREI SEMIONOVICH: Petia! Let's make a deal: I'll give you something, and you give me my arm back.

PETR PAVLOVICH: No, I won't give you your arm back. Don't bother asking. But if you like, we'll go to Professor Tartarelin, he'll cure you.

[ANDREI SEMIONOVICH *jumped with joy and went to see* PROFESSOR TARTARELIN.]

ANDREI SEMIONOVICH: Most honorable Professor, please cure my right arm. It was torn off by my acquaintance, Petr Pavlovich, and he will not give it back to me.

Petr Pavlovich were standing in the professor's foyer, exploding with demonic laughter. Tucked in His armpit was the arm of Andrei Semionovich, which He held with distaste, rather like a briefcase.

Having examined Andrei Semionovich's shoulder, the professor lit a pipe-cigarette and muttered: "It's an inshhury."

ANDREI SEMIONOVICH: Excuse me, what were you saying?
PROFESSOR: An inshhury.
ANDREI SEMIONOVICH: Injury?
PROFESSOR: Yes, yes, yes. An inshhury. Im-shhoo-ree!
ANDREI SEMIONOVICH: A fine injury, when there's no arm to speak of!

[*Laughter is heard from the foyer.*]

PROFESSOR: Oh! Who's that lathhing?
ANDREI SEMIONOVICH: That's nothing at all. Don't you worry about it.
PROFESSOR: Ho! Wish pleashure. How would you like it if we read something?

ANDREI SEMIONOVICH: How about you cure me.

PROFESSOR: Yes, yes, yes. Let's read a little, and later I'll cure you. Have a seat.

[*They sit down.*]

PROFESSOR: Would you like me to read to you from my science?

ANDREI SEMIONOVICH: Please! That's very interesting.

PROFESSOR: Only I've written it in verse.

ANDREI SEMIONOVICH: That's very interesting indeed!

PROFESSOR: Here we are, hah-hah, I'll read to you from here to there. This here is about internal organs. And here it tells of joints.

PETR PAVLOVICH [*entering the room*]:

Zdygr appr oostr oostr
I have in hand another's arm
zdygr appr oostr oostr
where's Professor Tartarelin?
zdygr appr oostr oostr
where's the office hour clock?
if these dingalingy thingies
with two dumbbells to the floor
the old lady's little watches
traced a parabola in flight
zdygr appr oostr oostr
I've spoiled the motion of the clock
in its stead the karabistr
on a doily zdygr appr
with an arm of endlessness
employed as arrows
from one minute to the next
rushes as if burned by fire

under the white face of the clock
a pancake winds up oostr oostr
tucked into a robe of terry cloth
the karabistr sits enthroned
and he watches office seconds
through an engine marked and measured
so that time won't go astray
where Professor Tartarelin
Andrei Semionych zdygr
the one-armed one zdygr appr
cures the zdygr appr oostr
reaffixes arm to shoulder
hammers fingers into place
zdygr appr oostr hammers
zdygr appr oostr beats

PROFESSOR TARTARELIN: Was it you who mutilated this citizen, Petr Pavlovich?

PETR PAVLOVICH: I tore his arm right out of the sleeve.

ANDREI SEMIONOVICH: Then he ran after me.

PROFESSOR: Answer the question!

[PETR PAVLOVICH *laughs.*]

KARABISTR: Gvindaleyah!

PETR PAVLOVICH: Karabistr!

KARABISTR: Gvindalan!

PROFESSOR: Tell me how it happened.

ANDREI SEMIONOVICH:

Just a little while ago
through the fields I took a stroll
and suddenly who do I see
calmly coming toward me

well if it isn't Petia,
and as if he doesn't notice
he tries to slip by.
I yelled at him: Ah, Petia!
Hello, Petia, my acquaintance,
it seems you didn't notice
me approaching.

PETR PAVLOVICH:

But the lord of circumstance
and the crossing of events
from the dawn of time to now
governs us, like children,
starves us in the desert,
and whips us in the room.

PROFESSOR: So it is, that's understood. The confluence of circumstances. That's the truth. A law.

At this point, Petr Pavlovich leaned over toward the professor and
bit off his ear. Andrei Semionovich ran for the police, while Petr
Pavlovich threw Andrei Semionovich's arm on the floor, placed
Professor Tartarelin's bitten-off ear on the table, and left incon-
spicuously by the back stairway.

Professor Tartarelin lay on the floor and moaned.

"Oh-oh-oh, it hurts!" moaned the professor. "My wound burns
and pours forth juices. Where is a compassionate man to be found
who would wash my wound and fill it with collodion?!"

It was a marvelous night. The stars, positioned in the sky according to their fixed patterns, shone down from far above. Breathing
with his whole chest, Andrei Semionovich dragged two policemen
to the home of Professor Tartarelin. Waving his only arm, Andrei
Semionovich related the events that had unfolded.

One of the policemen asked Andrei Semionovich:

"What is the name of this stranger?"

Andrei Semionovich did not turn in his comrade, and didn't even give his name.

Then both policemen asked Andrei Semionovich:

"Tell us, have you known him long?"

"Since my youngest years, when I was only so big," said Andrei Semionovich.

"What does he look like?" asked the policemen.

"His most notable feature is a long black beard," said Andrei Semionovich.

The policemen stopped, pulled their hats tight over their heads and, opening their mouths wide, sang in drawn-out nocturnal voices:

> Oh, how interesting and weird,
> once his friend was young,
> but when the friend grew up
> he began to wear a beard.

"You possess quite passable voices. Permit me to express my gratitude," said Andrei Semionovich, and extended an empty sleeve to the policemen, because he had no arm.

"We can even hold a conversation on scientific matters," said the policemen in unison.

Andrei Semionovich waved his blank sleeve in disbelief.

"The earth has seven oceans," began the policemen. "The scientific physicists studied sunspots and brought themselves to the conclusion that there was no hydrogen on the planets and any cohabitation would be inappropriate there.

"In our atmosphere there exists such a point that whups any center.

"The English crematorium Albert Einstein invented a machination through which any thingamajig is relative."

"Oh gracious policemen!" intoned Andrei Semionovich. "Let us make haste, or else my friend will kill Professor Tartarelin once and for all."

One of the policemen was called Volodia, the other was called Seriozha. Volodia took Seriozha by the arm and Seriozha grabbed Andrei Semionovich by the sleeve, and the three of them ran on together.

"Look there, three coeds!" yelled the carriage drivers as they passed. One of them even snapped Seriozha on the fanny with his whip.

"Hold it! On my way back I'll fine you for that!" yelled Seriozha, never letting Andrei Semionovich out of his grasp.

When they reached the professor's house, all three said "Tprrr!" and halted.

"By the stairs, to the third floor!" commanded Andrei Semionovich.

"*Hoch!*" cried the policemen and rushed up the stairs.

Using their shoulders to force open the door, they burst into Professor Tartarelin's office.

Professor Tartarelin sat on the floor, while the professor's wife stood on her knees before him sewing on his ear with a thread of pink silk. The professor held a pair of scissors in his hands. He was cutting open his wife's dress around the belly. When the wife's naked belly appeared, the professor rubbed it with his hand and peered into it as though it were a mirror.

"Watch where you're sewing! Don't you see that one ear came out higher than the other?" said the professor in an angry voice.

His wife tore off the ear and began sewing it on anew.

The woman's naked belly clearly made a happy impression on the professor. His mustache bristled and his eyes smiled wide.

"Katia," said the professor, "forget sewing the ear over on the side. It would be much better if you sewed it to my cheek."

Katia, the wife of Professor Tartarelin, patiently tore off the ear a second time and began sewing it to the professor's cheek.

"Oh, that tickles so! Ha-ha-ha! How it tickles!" laughed the professor, but, noticing the policemen standing in the doorway, he suddenly became silent and put on a serious face.

OFFICER SERIOZHA: Where is the victim?

OFFICER VOLODIA: Whose ear has been bitten off?

PROFESSOR [*rising to his feet*]: Gentlemen! I am a man who has studied the sciences for fifty-six years, thank God, and do not meddle in other affairs. If you think that my ear has been bitten off, then you are cruelly mistaken. As you can see, both my ears are intact. Granted, one of them is on my cheek, but such is my will.

OFFICER SERIOZHA: Indeed, that is true, both ears are present and accounted for.

OFFICER VOLODIA: My cousin's eyebrows grew under his nose in a similar fashion.

KARABISTR: Fasfalakation!

PROFESSOR: Office hours are over.

PROFESSOR'S WIFE: It's time for bed!

ANDREI SEMIONOVICH: It's half past eleven.

POLICEMEN [*in unison*]: Good night.

ECHO: Sweet dreams.

[*The* PROFESSOR *lies down on the floor. The others also lie down and fall asleep.*]

THE DREAM

quietly the ocean splashes
the looming cliffs cry doo doo doo
quietly the ocean flashes
a man is singing through a flute
quietly over the sea
run white elephants of fear
the slippery fish sing
the stars fall off the moon
a feeble house stands
its doors wide open
its warm stoves beckon
watchmen sleep in the house
on the roof a woman dozes
and on her crooked nose is
an ear splashing quiet wind
blowing hair around all things
and a cuckoo in the branches
gazes northward through its glasses
do not gaze my cuckoo darling
don't gaze northward all night long
only the wind of karabistr
keeps the time in numbers there
only the falcon of sdygr oostr
lies in wait there for his prey

PETR PAVLOVICH:

Someone's asleep in this dusky lair,
I grope and sniff: a table, a chair,
I bump into an old commode,
I see the tree of bergamot,
in a hurry I pick a pear—

71

what the devil! It's an ear!
I'm afraid, I run to the right,
before me stands a sapling grove,
I run back, first to then fro,
bumping into the frame of the door,
my legs buckled and downward drove,
I thought: the doors are actually a stove,
I jumped to the left—a bed I found,
help, help! . . .

PROFESSOR [*waking up*]: What's that sound?

ANDREI SEMIONOVICH [*leaping to his feet*]: Phew! What a dream I had, as if all our ears were torn off. [*Turns on the light.*]

As it turns out, while everyone was sleeping, Petr Pavlovich came around and cut everybody's ears off.

SERIOZHA the policeman remarks:
"A dream come true!"

March–April 1929
Translated by Matvei Yankelevich

The Ewe

1

The white ewe walked
the white ewe wandered
cried out in the fields above the river
called for its lambs and minor birds
waved its white hand
lay prostrate before me
invited me into the grass
and in the grass waving its hand
the white ewe walked
the white ewe wandered.

2

Do you know the white ewe
do you believe the white ewe
stands in its crowns by the stove
the same identical as you
As if I were friends with you
as if it were bright crowns I held
you are above us and then I
and then a house on three pillars
and higher yet the white ewe
walks the white ewe.

3

The white ewe walks
and after her the capricorn
with a big face among the saints
with a purse hirsute like the earth
stands in the pasture like a house
the earth below, thunder above
we to the side, earth all around
and God above among the saints
and higher yet the white ewe
walks the white ewe.

May 22, 1929
Translated by Eugene Ostashevsky

Thing

Mama, Papa, and domestic help entitled Natasha were sitting at the dinner table and drinking.

Papa was a boozehound, no doubt about it. Even Mama looked down on him. But this did not prevent Papa from being a very nice person. He was laughing very genially and rocking in his chair. The maid Natasha, who wore a headpiece and an apron, was blushing in unbelievable embarrassment. Papa was making everyone laugh with his beard, but the maid Natasha bashfully lowered her eyes to demonstrate her embarrassment thereby.

Mama, a tall woman with big hair, spoke with the voice of a horse. Mama's voice trumpeted in the dining room, reverberating throughout the apartment and into the yard.

After the first round, everyone fell silent for a moment and ate some cold cuts. A short while later they started talking again.

Then, out of nowhere, someone knocked at the door. Neither Papa, nor Mama, nor the maid Natasha had any idea who it could possibly be.

"How strange," said Papa. "Who could be knocking at the door?"

Mama made a sympathetic face and poured an extra shot for herself, drank it and said: "Strange."

Papa refrained from comment, but he poured himself a shot as well. He drank it and rose from the table.

In height, Papa was nothing to look at. No comparison with Mama. Mama was a tall, full-bodied woman with a voice like a horse, whereas Papa was only her spouse. Moreover, Papa had freckles.

He got to the door in one step and asked: "Who's there?"

"It's me," said the voice behind the door.

Right then the door opened and the maid Natasha walked in, self-conscious and pink. Just like a flower. Just like a flower.

Papa sat down.

Mama drank some more.

The maid Natasha and the other one, the one just like a flower, turned red with shame. Papa looked at them and refrained from comment, except that he drank another shot, as did Mama.

To silence the unpleasant burning in his mouth, Papa opened a can of lobster pâté. Everyone was very happy and ate until dawn. But Mama sat in her seat saying nothing. This wasn't pleasant at all.

Just as Papa was about to sing something, there was a bang on the window. Mama jumped up afraid and screamed that she clearly saw someone looking into the window from the street. The others tried to reassure her, saying this was impossible, insofar as the apartment was on the third floor. No one could have looked in from the street, you'd have to be a giant for that, or Goliath.

But the thought was firmly lodged inside Mama's head. Nothing in the world could have convinced her that nobody had looked through the window.

To calm her down, they poured her another shot. She drank it. Papa also poured one for himself and drank it.

Natasha and the maid who was just like a flower were sitting with their eyes lowered in embarrassment.

"I can't be in a good mood when we are being looked at through the window!" Mama was shouting.

Papa grew desperate. He had no idea how to reassure Mama. He ran down into the yard and tried to look from there into the windows of at least the second story. Of course, he was unable to reach even that high up. But Mama was not convinced by this at all. Mama never even saw that Papa failed to reach the windows of even the second story.

Papa blew into the dining room in great frustration and immediately gulped down two shots, pouring an extra one for Mama. Mama drank it but announced she was drinking merely out of conviction that someone had, in fact, looked in through the window.

Papa threw up his arms.

"Look," he said to Mama, and, approaching the window, pulled both frames ajar.

A man with a soiled shirt collar and a knife in his hands tried to climb in. Papa slammed the window shut and said: "There's no one there."

But the man with the soiled shirt collar was standing outside the window and staring into the room. He even opened the window and walked in.

Mama became awfully excited. She fell into a fit of hysterics, but, after drinking a bit of what Papa offered her and chasing it down with a marinated mushroom, she calmed down again.

Soon Papa too returned to his senses. Everyone sat back down at the table and went on drinking.

Papa picked up a newspaper and turned it around several times, trying to figure out which end is the top and which the bottom. But he didn't succeed no matter how hard he tried, and so set the paper aside for another drink.

"It's all good," said Papa, "but we're missing pickles."

Mama bellowed obscenely, which made the maids so embarrassed that they engrossed themselves in studying the patterns of the tablecloth.

Papa drank some more and then, snatching Mama, hoisted her up onto the wardrobe.

Mama's gray luxurious hairdo got knocked on its side, red splotches appeared on her face, and, all in all, she developed one excited mug.

Papa pulled up his pants and launched into a toast.

Just then a manhole in the floor opened, and a monk clambered out. The maids became so embarrassed that one of them even started to puke. Natasha propped her friend up by the forehead, trying to hide her disgraceful behavior.

The monk who clambered out from under the floorboards aimed at Papa's ear with his fist and then—wham!

Papa dropped back into his chair without finishing his toast.

Then the monk came up to Mama and hit her somehow from the bottom up—either with his hand, or with his foot, it was hard to tell.

Mama began to scream and call for help.

And the monk grabbed both maids by the collar, swung them in the air a bit, and let them go.

Then the monk hid back under the floorboards unnoticed and closed the manhole cover over his head.

For a long time Mama, Papa, and the maid Natasha could not come to their senses. But then, having caught their breath and straightened their clothes, they drank another round and sat back down at the table to eat pickled cabbage.

As they drank the next round, they sat around conversing peacefully.

But then Papa turned purple and started to yell.

"What! What!" Papa was shouting. "So you think I am petty! So I am a loser in your eyes! I'm no poor relative for you, I'm no mooch! You're scoundrels yourselves, that's what you are!"

Mama and the maid Natasha ran out of the dining room and locked themselves in the kitchen.

"He's going at it again, that boozehound! That old devil's hoof!" Mama was hissing in horror to Natasha who by now was as embarrassed as humanly possible.

And Papa sat shouting in the dining room until, in the morning, he picked up his folders, put on an official white cap, and went off modestly to work.

May 31, 1929
Translated by Eugene Ostashevsky

The Measure of Things

LIAPOLIANOV:

> You have a certain imperfection:
> under the floor you hide the inch,
> you make love to it like a flowery peach,
> at danger's approach you screech.

FRIENDS:

> We hold the inch dearer than eyesight,
> it's our measure for counting,
> it's our base in space,
> we're warriors of rectangular figures.
> We apply standards
> to measures of friable fluids,
> we pour mounds of tears on the ground,
> we span the forehead of our neighbor,
> who serves us for a hen.
> Examining the form of footprint
> we touch the measure with all our five.
> Curious about body heat
> of patients (also known as temperature),
> we carry them the inch.
> We make chicken from chicken soup.

LIAPOLIANOV:

> But physicists regard the inch
> as an outdated measure.

It's far handier
to measure objects with a saber.
It also fits to measure with your feet.

PROFESSOR GETTINCRETIN:

You are mistaken, Liapolianov.
It's me that am the representative of science
and I know things better than you do.
Feet measure fields,
the saber measures the human body,
but objects are measured by the fork.

FRIENDS:

We're mere infants when it comes to science,
but we do love the inch.

LIAPOLIANOV:

Death to outmoded measures!
Death to veterans of science!
Let wind drown the round islands!
Snap in half the robust meter!

CARPENTER:

No, no,
excuse me.
I know the slanting fathom
and I don't give a damn for your inventions!
It being that the fathom
is slanting in the capacity of instrument
and capable of application
in any situation:
for instance, at the building of a house
take a fathom weight of bricks,
plaster and straw
and the heavy hammer.

PROFESSOR GETTINCRETIN:

> Here we are,
> staring at the ceiling
> discussing the calibration
> of assorted levels of nature
> undergoing transformation
> from energy to basic matter,
> under which we signify
> even gas.

FRIENDS:

> We concealed our measure.
> We prefer the inch to eyesight, yes!

LIAPOLIANOV:

> In every little particle
> in elements
> in angels
> in points of convergence
> in flying cannonballs
> in surfaces
> in tensions
> in pits of spiritual boredom
> in bubbles of logical science,
> what is it that measures objects?
> It's the wedge, the beak, the fang.

PROFESSOR GETTINCRETIN:

> You're mistaken, Liapolianov.
> Where did you hear that nonsense:
> Measure the chair with the wedge?
> Measure the table with the beak?
> Measure the key with the lyre?
> Net the house with an oath?

We walk in science with the meter,
all you carry is a saber.

LIAPOLIANOV:

Listen to how I reckon now:
There isn't any measure.
There are, instead of measure,
our thoughts encased in objects.
All the objects come alive,
making Being attractive.

FRIENDS:

Oh,
we got it!
Still,
we stick to the Inch.

LIAPOLIANOV:

Boneheads.

PROFESSOR GETTINCRETIN:

Ignoramuses and fools.

CARPENTER:

I won't be friends with you anymore.

That's all.

October 17–21, 1929
Translated by Eugene Ostashevsky

The Saber

I

Life is divided into work time and free time. Free time creates schemas—that is, pipes. Work time fills these pipes.

> Work in the form of wind
> Flies into a hollow pipe.
> The pipe sings in a lazy voice.
> We listen to the howl of pipes.
> And our body is suddenly lighter
> and transforms into beautiful wind;
> suddenly we become double:
> to the right, a little hand—
> to the left, a little hand,
> to the right, a little foot—
> to the left, a little foot,
> our sides, our ears, our eyes, our shoulders
> make boundaries between us with the rest.
> Just like rhymes our edges
> shine like steel blades.

2

Free time is an empty pipe. In our free time we lie on the couch, smoke and drink lots, visit friends, talk a lot, making excuses for ourselves to each other. We make excuses for our actions, separate ourselves from everything else and say that we have the right to an independent existence. Then we start imagining that we own everything that is outside of us. And all that exists outside of us, and which is separated by boundaries from us and everything else that differs from us and its (that, of which we are speaking at this very moment) space (even if it's just air), we call an object. We separate out the object into an autonomous world, and it begins to own everything that lies outside of it, just as we do.

Autonomously existing objects are no longer tied down by the laws of logical sequence and hop around in space wherever they like, just as we do. Words in the noun category also hop around, following after objects. Nouns beget verbs and bestow upon them the freedom of choice. Following nouns, objects carry out various actions, as free as the new verb. New qualities arise, and, after them, free adjectives. So matures a new generation of parts of speech. Speech that is free of the ruts of logic runs along new paths, bounded off from other speech. The edges of speech shine a bit brighter, so that one can see the end and the beginning. Otherwise, we'd get totally lost. These edges fly, like breezes, into the empty verse-pipe. The pipe starts to sound, and we hear rhyme.

3

Hooray! Poems have outrun us!
We are not free like poems.
In the pipe we hear the wind's voice,
While we are silent and weak.
Where is the boundary of our bodies,
Where are our bright sides?
We are vague as gossamer,
We are helpless for now.

> Words and speech are soaring fast,
> Objects ride in pursuit,
> And we fight in the fray—
> We shout to victories: Hooray!

In this way, we get wrapped up in the working state. There's no time for thoughts of food and guests. Conversations no longer justify our actions: in the midst of a fight you don't ask for forgiveness or justification. Now everyone fends for himself. Everyone puts himself into motion by his own will and passes right through the others. Everything existing outside of us has ceased being a part of us. We no longer resemble the world that surrounds us. The world flies into our mouths in the form of separate bits and pieces: rock, amber, glass, iron, wood, etc. Coming up to a table, we say: this is a table, not I, so take that!—and we bash our fist on the table, and the table breaks in two; and we bash the halves, and the halves break up into powder; and we bash the powder, and the powder flies into our mouth; and we say: this is dust, not I—and bash the dust. But dust is not afraid of our blows.

4

We stand here and say: now I've stretched out one arm in front of me, and the other arm behind me. And now, in front, I end where my arm ends, and in back I also end where my arm ends. On top, I end with the top of my head, on the bottom with my heels, and on the sides with my shoulders. Now, this is all of me, and whatever is outside me, is not me anymore.

Now, when we've become completely independent, let's polish our edges, so that it becomes easier to see where begins that which is not us anymore. We polish the bottom point—the boots. The topmost point—the top of the head—we mark with a hat. We'll put shiny cuffs on our arms and epaulets on our shoulders. Now it's easy to see where we end and everything else begins.

5

The three pairs of our edges are as follows:

1. arm—arm.
2. shoulder—shoulder.
3. head—heels.

6

QUESTION: Has our work begun? And if it has, of what does it consist?

ANSWER: Our work will begin soon and consists of the registration of the world, because now we are no longer the world.

Q: But if we are not the world, then what are we?

A: No, we are the world. That is, I did not express myself correctly. It's not that we are no longer the world, but we are by ourselves, and it is by itself. I can clarify: there exist numbers—1, 2, 3, 4, 5, 6, 7, etc. All these numbers make up the natural, or countable, number sequence. Any number will find a place here. But 1 is a special number. It can stand to the side as a sign of the absence of count. Two is already the first multiple, and after 2 come all the other numbers. Some savages know how to count only like this: one and many. Such are we in the world, like ones in the natural number sequence.

Q: All right, but how are we going to go about registering the world?

A: The same way the one registers the other numbers, that is, by fitting into them and observing what comes of it.

Q: Is that really the way the one registers other numbers?

A: Let's say it is. It's not important.

Q: That's odd. And how are we going to fit ourselves into other objects placed in the world? Observing how much wider, deeper, and taller a wardrobe is compared to ourselves? Is that it?

A: We represent the one by using a sign in the form of a little stick. The sign of the number one is simply the most convenient form for the representation of the one, as is any number sign. In the same way, we are only the most convenient form of ourselves.

The one, registering the two, does not fit its sign into the sign of two. The one registers numbers by means of its quality. And we should do the same.

Q: But what is our quality?

A: Death of the ear—
   loss of hearing,
   death of the nose—
   loss of nearing,
   death of the throat—
   loss of speech,
   death of the eye—
   loss of seech.

We also know the abstract quality of the number one. But the concept of one exists within us as the concept of something. A yard, let's say. One registers two—so it is: one yard fits into two yards, one matchstick fits into two matchsticks, etc. There are many such ones. Likewise, a person is not one but many. And we have as many qualities as there are people. And each of us has his own special quality.

Q: What quality do I have?

A: Exactly. Our work must begin with the discovery of our own quality. Because we will arm ourselves with this quality, let us call it a *weapon.*

Q: But how shall I find my weapon?

7

If there are no longer any means
to conquer the flood of meanings,
one must leave the battle proudly
and take up one's peaceful tasks.
Peaceful is the task of building a house
out of logs with the aid of an ax.
I went out into the world deafened by thunder.
A mountain of houses spread before me.
But the saber, my singular flesh,
whistling leftover of war,
cleaves swallows from the roofs
unable to hack through a log.
Shall I exchange my weapon or my task?
Shall I slash my enemies or build my house?
Or rip the lace from maid from oak
and plunge my saber in their breast?
I am a carpenter armed with a saber,
I meet the house as though a foe.
The house stands stricken through the center
bowing its horns to the floor.
Here is my saber, my measure
my feather, my faither, my failure!

APPENDIX
8

Kozma Prutkov registered the world from the Assay Office, which meant that he was armed with a saber.[*]

The following all had sabers: Goethe, Blake, Lomonosov, Gogol, Prutkov, and Khlebnikov. Having received a saber, one can set out upon his task and register the world.

9

The registration of the world.
(Saber = measure)[†]

That's all.

November 19–20, 1929
Translated by Matvei Yankelevich

---

[*] Kozma Prutkov's dream: A naked general. It's good that the general had epaulets, but it's too bad that he didn't hand down his saber to Prutkov.

[†] "Time is the measure of the world."—Velimir Khlebnikov

Notnow

This is This.
That is That.
This is not That.
This is not This.
What's left is either this, or not this.
It's all either that, or not that.
What's not that and not this, that is not this and not that.
What is this and also that, that is itself Itself.
What is itself Itself, that might be that but not this, or else
    this but not that.
This went into that, and that went into this. We say: God
    has puffed.
This went into this, and that went into that, and we have no
    place to leave and nowhere to come to.
This went into this. We asked: where? They sung in answer:
    Here.
This left That. What is this? It's That.
This is that.
That is this.
Here are this and that.
Here went into this, this went into that, and that went into
    here.
We watched but did not see.
And there stood this and that.

There is not here.
That's there.
This is here.
But now both this and that are there.
But now this and that are here, too.
We long and mope and ponder.
But where is now?
Now is here, and now there, and now here, and now here
    and there.
This be that.
Here be there.
This, that, here, there, be, I, We, God.

May 29, 1930
Translated by Matvei Yankelevich

To Ring—To Fly
(Third Cisfinite Logic)

I

And now the house flew.
And now the dog flew.
And now the dream flew.
And now the mother flew.
And now the garden flew.
The horse flew.
The bathhouse flew.
The balloon flew.
Now the rock starts to flying.
Now the stump starts to flying.
Now the moment starts to flying.
Now the circle starts to flying.
A house flies.
A mother flies.
A garden flies.
A clock to fly.
A hand to fly.
Eagles to fly.
A spear to fly.
And horse to fly.
And house to fly.

And period to fly.
A forehead flies.
A chest flies.
A stomach flies.
Oh-no, catch it—the ear is flying.
Oh-no, look—the nose is flying.
Oh-no, my monks—the mouth is flying.

2

The house rings.
The water rings.
The rock nearby is ringing.
The book nearby is ringing.
Mother, son, and garden ring.
A rings.
B rings.
THAT flies and THAT rings.
The forehead rings and flies.
The chest rings and flies.
Hey, monks—mouth is ringing!
Hey, monks—forehead's flying!
What to fly, but not to ring?
The ring is flying and to ring.
THERE is flying and ringing.
Hey, monks! We're to fly!
Hey, monks! We're to flying! We're to fly and THERE to fly.
Hey, monks! We're to ringing!
We're to ringing and THERE to ring.

Spring 1930
Translated by Matvei Yankelevich

The Werld

I told myself that I see the world. But the whole world was not accessible to my gaze, and I saw only parts of the world. And everything that I saw I called parts of the world. And I examined the properties of these parts and, examining these properties, I wrought science. I understood that the parts have intelligent properties and that the same parts have unintelligent properties. I distinguished them and gave them names. And, depending on their properties, the parts of the world were intelligent or unintelligent.

And there were such parts of the world as could think. And these parts looked upon me and upon the other parts. And all these parts resembled one another, and I resembled them. And I spoke with these parts.

I said: parts thunder.

The parts said: a clump of time.

I said: I am also part of the three turns.

The parts answered: And we are little points.

And suddenly I ceased seeing them and, soon after, the other parts as well. And I was frightened that the world would collapse.

But then I understood that I do not see the parts independently, but I see it all at once. At first I thought that it was NOTHING. But then I understood that this was the world and what I had seen before was not the world.

And I had always known what the world was, but what I had seen before I do not know even now.

And when the parts disappeared, their intelligent properties ceased being intelligent, and their unintelligent properties ceased being unintelligent. And the whole world ceased to be intelligent and unintelligent.

But as soon as I understood that I saw the world, I ceased seeing it. I became frightened, thinking that the world had collapsed. But while I was thinking this, I realized that had the world collapsed then I would already not be thinking this. And I watched, looking for the world, but not finding it.

And soon after there wasn't anywhere to look.

Then I realized that, while I had somewhere to look, there had been a world around me. And now it's gone. There's only me.

And then I realized that I am the world.

But the world—is not me.

Although at the same time I am the world.

But the world's not me.

And I am the world.

But the world's not me.

And I am the world.

But the world's not me.

And I am the world.

And, after that, I didn't think anything more.

May 30, 1930
Translated by Matvei Yankelevich

An Evening Song to She Who Exists by My Name

Daughter of the daughter of the daughters of the daughter Pe
foreto the apple you ate of yee
beguiling Adam's heights foreto you favorite daughter of the
daughter of Pe
being the Mother of the world and the world itself and the
child of the world being
open the eye of the soul of grain
open the shores and do not turn yee head about
open the fallen shadows of thrones to the larch
open through Angels singing birds
open the sighing breath in the air of the sown winds
that call you down to them that call you
that love you
that yellow find yee in life.

The steam bath of your faces
the steam bath of your faces
foreto opening memory's window take a look around what is
situated in the distance
take a count of the moving and the restless
and count out on your hand α those restless ones
those restless ones foreto taking from movement accepting
life

long to move and yet still sleeputh
or quick say: from movement comes life
but in stillness death.

Origin and Power will fit into thy shoulder
Origin and Power will fit into thy forehead
Origin and Power will fit into the sole of thy foot
but you will never take fire and arrow into your hand
but you will never take fire and arrow into your hand
foreto the ladder of thou head
daughter of the daughter of the daughters of the daughter
of Pe

O fy lily of mine eyes
fe the inkwell of mine cheeks
trrr the ear of mine hair
quill of happiness reflection of the light of mine things
key of ashes and bosom of flowing pride
take cover in silence people of this mine country
foreto wink number height and horse's ride

Of willfulness shall we sing sister
of willfulness shall we sing sister
daughter of the daughter of the daughters of Pe
name-day girl of your own name
of your own legs the wind and of your own bosom the bee
of your own hands the strength and my breath
uneasyseeable depth of my soul
the light that sings in my city
joy of the night and forest of the graveyard of stillstanding
times

with courage come into the world and life's witness
come to me in my dreams.

August 21, 1930
Translated by Matvei Yankelevich

The Daughter of Patruliov

I would like to tell you about an incident involving a fish, or rather not even a fish, but a man named Patruliov, or, to be even more precise, the daughter of Patruliov.

I will begin with her birth. Speaking of birth: right on our wooden floor there were born . . . No, we can talk about that later.

Let's get to the point:

The daughter of Patruliov was born on a Saturday. Let us designate the daughter by the Latin letter M.

Having designated the daughter by the Latin letter M, let us note that:

1. Around the boots go two hands and two foots.
2. In some ways the ears are the same as the eyes.
3. To run is an underfooted verb.
4. To feel is an underhanded verb.
5. Only the son can wear a mustache.
6. The back of your head can't see what hangs on the wall.
17. Note that seventeen comes right after six.

In order to color in the picture, let us remember these seventeen postulates.

Now let's place our hand on the fifth postulate and see what happens.

If we had placed a cart on the fifth postulate—or sugar, or a natural ribbon—then we would have been forced to admit: yes, and something besides that.

But let us in fact imagine, and for simplicity's sake immediately forget what we just imagined.

Now let's look at what happened.

You look over here while I look over here, and the result will be that both of us are looking over there.

Or, to be more precise, I am looking there while you are looking elsewhere.

Now let's determine what it is that we see. It suffices to determine separately what it is that I see, and what it is that you see.

I see one half of the house, and you see the other half of the city. For simplicity's sake, let's call it: a wedding.

Now let's proceed with the daughter of Patruliov. Her wedding took place, let's say, at such and such a date. If her wedding had taken place earlier, then we would have said that her wedding had taken place prematurely. If her wedding had taken place later, then we would have said, "It's a wave," because the wedding had taken place later.

All seventeen postulates, otherwise known as feathers, are present and accounted for. Let's proceed to the following.

> The following is thicker than the preceding.
> The catfish is thicker than the oil-stove.
> The propeller screw is thicker than the onion.
> The book is thicker than the notebook,
> whereas notebooks are thicker than one notebook.
> This is a table, it is thicker than the book.
> This is a vault, it is thicker than the floor.
> This table is thicker than the preceding one,
> and the preceding one is taller than the onion.

The onion is smaller than the comb
in the same way as the hat is smaller than the child's bed
in which a box of books
can be placed,
but the box
is deeper than the hat.
The hat is softer
than the propeller screw,
but the bee is sharper than the sphere.
What grows on this
and on the other side of the fence
is equally beautiful.
Still, the book is more flexible than soup.
The ear is more flexible than the book.
The soup is more watery and has more fat than the wood
    chip
and is heavier than the key.

Assertion:

Rabbits have arms in place of mustaches.
Papa has a pheasant at the back of his head.
The store has four thumbtacks.
The rosalia has a dandelion.
The dog has a macanash.
The newspaper has eight signs.
I have a tail.
You have a crib.
The giants have a hat.

Combination:

House with beak.
Infant with Tatar.
Sea captain in kerosene.

Plate without hair.
Crow among passable numbers.
Fur coat with noise named Fofa.
Kalya at a dead end.
A Romanian from the washstand.
The angel Yershov.

Flight:

The rooster ran out of the water.
Jean ran out of the beard.
The nail ran out of the paraffin.
The whip jumped out of the carafe.
The sword ran out of the cockroach.
The experience rode out from under the glass.
The astronomer ran out of cotton.
The oblong key lay.

Combination:

House with beak.
Infant with Tatar.
Sea captain in kerosene.
Plate without hair.
Crow among passable numbers.
Fur coat with noise named Fofa.
Kalya at a dead end.
A Romanian from the washstand.
The angel Yershov.

Meditation:

This is not a forge but a bucket.
This is not rice but a ruler.
This is not a glove but the warehouse supervisor.
This is not an eye but the knee.

It was not I who came but you.
This is not water but tea.
This is not a nail but a screw.
And the screw is not a nail.
Fur is not the same as light.
A man with one arm is not the same as a room with one
    window.
Slippers are not toenails.
Slippers are not kidneys.
Neither are they nostrils.

Conclusions:

The daughter of Patruliov the father is the daughter of
    Patruliov,
Therefore also the daughter of Patruliov is the daughter of
    father Patruliov.
In that case also the daughter of the father Patruliov

Is therefore also the daughter of Patruliov father.
Here is the daughter, her father is Patruliov
Patruliov's daughter, the father is Patruliov
Therefore Patruliov is the father of Patruliov's
    daughter
And no one would say he is Petukhov
That just wouldn't be natural.

1930
Translated by Eugene Ostashevsky

Before Coming to See You

Before coming to see you I will knock on your window. You will see me in the window. Then I will stand in the doorway and you will see me in the doorway. Then I will come into your house and you will recognize me. Then I will enter you and no one, apart from you, will see me or know who I am.

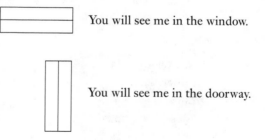

You will see me in the window.

You will see me in the doorway.

1931
Translated by Eugene Ostashevsky

The Constancy of Dirt and Joy

Cool water gurgles in the river,
mountain shadows lie down in a field,
and in the sky the light fades, while
birds have flown into our dreams,
and the janitor with his black mustache
stands all night long by the rusty gate
and with his dirty hands he scratches
under his dirty hat his itching pate,
through windows hear the joyous din,
the stomp of feet and bottles' ring.

A day goes by, and then a week,
and then the years are passing by,
and one by one in single file
the people vanish in their graves,
while the janitor with his black mustache
stands all night long by the rusty gate
and with his dirty hands he scratches
under his dirty hat his itching pate,
through windows hear the joyous din,
the stomp of feet and bottles' ring.

The moon and sun have paled together,
the constellations change their shape,
and motion turns to sticky syrup,

and time becomes a lot like sand.
Still the janitor with his black mustache
stands all night long by the rusty gate
and with his dirty hands he scratches
under his dirty hat his itching pate,
through windows hear the joyous din,
the stomp of feet and bottles' ring.

October 14, 1933
Translated by Matvei Yankelevich

An American Story

An American court received the complaint of a slaughterhouse guard that some guy broke his arm. The judge summoned this guy and asked him: "Did you break the guard's arm?" The guy said, "No, I didn't break his arm." But the guard said, "What do you mean, you didn't break my arm? I broke my arm because of you!" Then the judge said, "Explain what happened." This, as it turned out, is what happened:

A big young guy snuck into the slaughterhouse, cut a teat off a cow's udder, stuck it out through his fly and went off.

The guard saw the guy, his eyes popped out, and he says, "Just look at how you're walking around!"

But the guy took out his knife and says, "Ah, I don't care!" Then he cut off the teat and threw it aside.

The guard fell down and broke his arm.

January 1934
Translated by Eugene Ostashevsky

Fenorov in America

[*An American street.* AMERICANS *are walking along the street. To the right is a ticket booth. The sign above the ticket booth reads,* MUSIC HALL, JAZZ ORCHESTRA UNDER THE DIRECTION OF MISTER WOOD-LEG AND HIS WIFE, THE BARONESS VON DER KLÜKEN. *Advertisements. A line of* AMERICANS *in front of the ticket booth.* FENOROV *enters and stares all around him. The* AMERICANS *have a rather ragged appearance.*]

FENOROV: So this must be it: America! . . . Yes sirree! America . . . Imagine that! . . . Hey, listen! . . . You! . . . Is this America?

AMERICAN: Ies, America.

FENOROV: And this is the city of Chicago?

AMERICAN: Ies, Chicago.

FENOROV: And you, then, are an American?

AMERICAN: An American.

FENOROV [*in a deep voice*]: Imagine that! . . . And those ones over there, are they Americans, too?

AMERICAN: Americans.

FENOROV [*in a falsetto*]: Woo hoo! . . . [*in a deeper voice*] Americans! . . . [*looking around*]. And so there are, I mean, you know, billionaires here as well?

AMERICAN: Why, there are as many as you'd like, my friend.

FENOROV: Then if, I mean, you're all billionaires and Americans, why are you walking around in clothes that are, you know, ragged?

AMERICAN: It's on account of the so-called crisis.

FENOROV [*in a falsetto*]: Woo hoo!

AMERICAN: What's true is true!

FENOROV [*in a deep voice*]: Now that's something!

AMERICAN: May I then ask who you might be?

FENOROV: Fenorov's my last name. As for my social class: I'm Khrentsch.

AMERICAN: Khre . . . What, *parlez-vous français?*

FENOROV [*in a falsetto*]: Say whah?

AMERICAN: *Vous parlez* in French?

FENOROV [*in a falsetto*]: Say whah?

AMERICAN: I said: you jabber in French?

FENOROV: What I can't I can't. As for American—that we speak as much as you wants. That we can! . . . But why don't you tell me, my good man, why's there a line here? What interesting thing are they giving away?

AMERICAN: This line is not for anything and they're not giving away anything very interesting. It's just a line for tickets.

FENOROV [*in a falsetto*]: Woo hoo!

AMERICAN: This, you know, is a music hall. Today there's a performance by the jazz orchestra of the renowned Mister Woodleg and his wife, the daughter of Baron von der Klüken.

FENOROV [*in a deep voice*]: Imagine that! . . . Thank you thank you thank you! I'm going to buy me a ticket [*he approaches the line*].

[*A long line of* AMERICANS *stands waiting at the ticket booth of the music hall.*]

FENOROV: Who's last?

GUY: Where you barging to? Get in line.

FENOROV: I just asked who was last in line.

GUY: You got a thing for asking, don't you?

FENOROV: Who's last? . . . [*touches the elbow of a* MISS].

MISS: Leave me alone! I'm standing behind this guy!

GUY: I'm not a guy for you, I'm the King of Mint Drops!

FENOROV [*in a falsetto*]: Woo hoo!

MISS: Well, la-di-da! I myself am the Queen of Dog Hair.

FENOROV [*in a deep voice*]: Now that's something!

GUY: Even if you are the Queen of Dog Hair, I couldn't care less!

MISS: You're a fine one to talk, mint drop!

GUY: You dog hair!

[*Circus number.*]

[*A fight in line. The* QUEEN OF DOG HAIR *is getting even with the* KING OF MINT DROPS. *Other* AMERICANS *are running around them, shouting:* "I'll bet she whips him!" "I'll bet he whips her!"]

[*Interior of the music hall. Both the stage and the auditorium are visible. The back doors of the auditorium open. Ragged* AMERICANS *rush in and take their seats amid shouting and yelling. Once seated, they freeze. The hall falls completely silent. The* MASTER OF CEREMONIES *comes on stage.*]

MASTER OF CEREMONIES: Ladies and gentlemen! We, as we are Americans, know how to have a good time. So here we are gathered for some fun. But how am I supposed to make you laugh, you devils you? You got your gum, you got your tobacco, and you just sit and spit, sit and spit . . . Could anything make you laugh? . . . Nah, no way! . . . That's just plain impossible!

AMERICANS: Gaw gaw gaw! . . . Gaw gaw gaw! We want to laugh.

MASTER OF CEREMONIES: But how do we do that? Do I know?

AMERICANS [*plaintively*]: Gaw gaw gaw!

MASTER OF CEREMONIES: You want me to make funny faces?

AMERICANS: We do, we do!

[MASTER OF CEREMONIES *makes a face.*]

AMERICANS [*laughing loudly*]: Hee hee hee . . . Oh that's funny! Oh
   oh oh that's funny!
MASTER OF CEREMONIES: Enough?
AMERICANS: More! More!
MASTER OF CEREMONIES: No, that's enough! Mister Woodleg's jazz
   orchestra will now perform for your listening pleasure!
AMERICANS [*applauding*]: Bravo! Bravo! Hurray! Hurray!
MASTER OF CEREMONIES: And in the orchestra, there's Mister
   Woodleg's wife, the Baroness von der Klüken, and their lovely
   children! [*Applause.*]

[*The* MASTER OF CEREMONIES *exits. Curtain. From the audience*
FENOROV'S *voice can be heard.*]

FENOROV: What's gonna happen now?
KING OF MINT DROPS [*jumping from his chair*]: Fellows, it's him
   again!
QUEEN OF DOG HAIR: Again that mint drop is raising a ruckus! [*The*
   KING *quickly sits down.*]
QUEEN [*threateningly*]: I'll get you!

[*The curtain rises.*]

1934
Translated by Thomas Epstein and Eugene Ostashevsky

Kolpakov, Braggart

There once lived a man named Fedor Fedorovich Kolpakov.

"I am not afraid," Fedor Fedorovich Kolpakov used to say, "of anything! Shoot me with cannons, throw me in the water, burn me with fire—I am not afraid of anything! I am not afraid of tigers, I am not afraid of eagles, I am not afraid of whales, I am not afraid of spiders—I am not afraid of anything!"

One time Fedor Fedorovich Kolpakov stood on a bridge watching divers dive into the water. He watched and he watched, and then, when the divers got out and took off their diving suits, he couldn't hold himself back and so he starts hollering at them.

"Hey," he's hollering, "that's nothing! I could do better than that! I am not afraid of anything! I am not afraid of tigers, I am not afraid of eagles, I am not afraid of whales, I am not afraid of spiders—I am not afraid of anything! Burn me with fire, shoot me with cannons, throw me in the water—I am not afraid of anything!"

"Oh yeah," say the divers, "you wanna try going underwater?"

"What for?" says Fedor Fedorovich and starts to leave.

"What are you, chicken?" say the divers.

"I am no chicken," says Fedor Fedorovich. "But why should I get under the water?"

"You're scared, that's what it is!" say the divers.

"No, I'm not scared!" says Fedor Fedorovich.

"Then put the suit on and get in the water."

So Fedor Fedorovich dove to the bottom. And the divers start hollering at him into the telephone from up top.

"So how is it going, Fedor Fedorovich? Scared?"

And Fedor Fedorovich answers them from below: "Niav . . . niav . . . niav . . ."

"OK," say the divers, "that's enough for him."

So they hauled Fedor Fedorovich out of the water, took off his diving suit, and Fedor Fedorovich is looking around him with his eyes all savage, and saying nothing but "Niav . . . niav . . . niav . . . o."

"There you go, man, don't go bragging," said the divers and put him down on the shore.

Fedor Fedorovich went home and never bragged ever again.

1934
Translated by Eugene Ostashevsky

Anton Antonovich Shaved Off His Beard

Anton Antonovich shaved off his beard and none of his acquaintances could recognize him any longer.

"How is that possible," Anton Antonovich exclaimed. "It's me, Anton Antonovich. It's just that I shaved off my beard."

"Yeah, right!" the acquaintances replied. "Anton Antonovich had a beard, and you don't."

"I am telling you, I too had a beard but I shaved it off!" Anton Antonovich insisted.

"All sorts of people had beards!" replied the acquaintances.

"What the hell is this, really," Anton Antonovich would say, losing his temper. "Who am I supposed to be then, according to you?"

"That we don't know," the acquaintances replied. "But you are not Anton Antonovich."

Stumped, Anton Antonovich could not decide what to do. He went to visit the Naskakovs, but they met him with expressions of astonishment, asking: "Who are you looking for?"

"I am looking for you, Marusia!" said Anton Antonovich. "Don't you know who I am?"

"No," said Marusia Naskakov. Her curiosity was piqued: "Wait . . . Maybe I saw you at Valentina Petrovna's?"

"What do you mean, Marusia?" said Anton Antonovich. "Look at me carefully. Do you recognize me?"

"Wait, wait . . . No, I can't recall who you are," said Marusia.

"I am Anton Antonovich, obviously!" said Anton Antonovich. "Do you recognize me now?"

"No," said Marusia. "You are joking."

1934–37
Translated by Eugene Ostashevsky

The Career
of Ivan Yakovlevich Antonov

This happened before the Revolution.

One merchant's wife yawned and a cuckoo flew into her mouth.

The merchant came running to the call of his spouse and, immediately comprehending what's what, acted very cleverly and courageously.

Thereby he achieved name recognition among the inhabitants of the town and they elected him senator.

But one evening after four years in the Senate the misfortunate merchant yawned and a cuckoo flew into his mouth.

His wife came running to the call of her spouse and then acted very cleverly and courageously.

Stories of her cleverness spread throughout the province, and the Metropolitan, wishing to meet her, had her brought to the capital.

As he listened to her long story, the Metropolitan yawned and a cuckoo flew into his mouth.

Ivan Yakovlevich Grigoriev came running to the loud call of the Metropolitan and then acted very cleverly and courageously.

In reward, Ivan Yakovlevich Grigoriev was renamed as Ivan Yakovlevich Antonov and presented to the Tsar.

And now the reason for the many promotions of Ivan Yakovlevich Antonov has become perfectly clear.

January 8, 1935
Translated by Eugene Ostashevsky

》》》 《《《

Holiday

On the roof of a certain building two draftsmen sat eating buckwheat kasha.

Suddenly one of the draftsmen shrieked with joy and took a long handkerchief out of his pocket. He had a brilliant idea—he would tie a twenty-kopeck coin into one end of the handkerchief and toss the whole thing off the roof down into the street and see what would come of it.

The second draftsman quickly caught on to the first one's idea. He finished his buckwheat kasha, blew his nose, and, having licked his fingers, got ready to watch the first draftsman.

As it happened, both draftsmen were distracted from the experiment with the handkerchief and twenty-kopeck coin. On the roof where both draftsmen sat an event occurred which could not have gone unnoticed.

The janitor Ibrahim was hammering a long stick with a faded flag into a chimney.

The draftsmen asked Ibrahim what it meant, to which Ibrahim answered: "This means that there's a holiday in the city."

"And what holiday would that be, Ibrahim?" asked the draftsmen.

"It's a holiday because our favorite poet composed a new poem," said Ibrahim.

And the draftsmen, shamed by their ignorance, dissolved into the air.

January 9, 1935
Translated by Matvei Yankelevich

The Street Incident

One man once jumped off a tram, except he did it so awkwardly that a car hit him.

The traffic stopped and the policeman set about determining the cause of the accident.

The driver was explaining something for a long time and pointing to the front wheels of his car.

The policemen felt the wheels and wrote something down in his book.

A fairly numerous crowd gathered.

Some citizen with dull eyes kept falling off a traffic stone.

Some lady repeatedly glanced at another lady who, in turn, repeatedly glanced at the former lady.

Then the crowd dispersed and the traffic started moving.

But the citizen with dull eyes still kept falling off the traffic stone until finally he too put a stop to this occupation.

At this time some man carrying what appeared to be a freshly bought chair became lodged under a moving tram.

Again the policeman came, again the crowd gathered, and the citizen with dull eyes again started falling off the traffic stone.

Well and later everything was all right again, and Ivan Semenovich Karpov even stopped by a self-service restaurant.

January 10, 1935
Translated by Eugene Ostashevsky

On the Death of Kazimir Malevich

Ripping the stream of memory,
You look around and your face is pride-stricken.
Your name is—Kazimir.
The sun of your salvation wanes and you look at it.
Beauty has supposedly torn apart your earth's mountains,
No area can frame your figure.
Give me those eyes of yours! I'll throw open a window in
  my head!
Man, why have you stricken your face with pride?
Your life is only a fly and your desire is succulent food.
No glow comes from the sun of your salvation.
Thunder will lay low the helmet of your head.
Pe—is the inkpot of your words.
Trr—is your desire.
Agalthon—is your skinny memory.
Hey, Kazimir! Where's your desk?
Looks as if it's not here, and your desire is—Trr.
Hey, Kazimir! Where's your friend?
She is also gone, and your memory's inkpot is—Pe.
Eight years have crackled away in those ears of yours.
Fifty minutes have beat away in that heart of yours.
Ten times has the river flowed before you.
The inkpot of your desire Trr and Pe has ended.

"Imagine that!" you say, and your memory is—Agalthon.
There you stand, pushing apart smoke with your hands
    supposedly.
The pride-stricken expression on that face of yours wanes,
And your memory and your desire Trr disappear.

May 5–17, 1935
Translated by Ilya Bernstein

One Fat Man

One fat man invented a way to lose weight. And he lost it. The ladies began pestering him, trying to pry out his secret. But the thin man replied that it becomes men to lose weight, whereas it does not become ladies at all; that ladies, on the contrary, ought to be plump. And he was absolutely right.

Mid-1930s
Translated by Eugene Ostashevsky

Death of a Little Old Man

A little sphere sprang out of one little old man's nose and fell to the ground. The little old man bent over to lift up the little sphere and that's when a little stick sprang from his eye and also fell to the ground. The little old man was frightened and, not knowing what to do, moved his lips. At that moment, out of the little old man's mouth sprang a little square. The little old man grabbed his mouth, but then a little mouse sprang out of the little old man's sleeve. The little old man became ill with fear and, so as not to fall, he sat down into a squat. But then something snapped inside the little old man and, like a soft plush coat, he toppled to the ground. That's when a longish little reed sprang from the torn hole, and on its very end sat a thin little bird. The little old man wanted to scream out, but one of his jaws got stuck behind the other and he only hiccupped weakly and closed one eye. The little old man's other eye remained open. It ceased moving and glistening and became motionless and murky, like that of a dead person. In such a way, cunning death caught up to the little old man who had not expected it.

1935–36
Translated by Matvei Yankelevich

The New Mountain Climbers

Bibikov climbed up a mountain, fell into deep thought, and rolled downward. The Chechens raised him up and again placed him on the summit. Bibikov thanked the Chechens and again rolled downward. That was the last they saw of him.

Next Aufgenapfel climbed up the mountain, looked through his binoculars, and saw a horseman.

"Hey," shouted Aufgenapfel. "Where's the restaurant around here?"

The horseman disappeared behind the mountain, then reappeared near the bushes, then disappeared behind the bushes, then reappeared in the valley, then disappeared behind the foot of the mountain, then reappeared on the slope and rode up to Aufgenapfel.

"Where's the restaurant around here?" asked Aufgenapfel.

The horseman pointed to his mouth and ears.

"What are you, deaf-mute?" asked Aufgenapfel.

The horseman scratched his head and pointed to his stomach.

"What are you saying?" asked Aufgenapfel.

The horseman took a wooden apple out of his pocket and bit it in half.

Aufgenapfel felt uneasy and stepped backward.

And the horseman took the boot off his foot and shouted, "Khal-ghallaj!"

Aufgenapfel bounced off to the side and rolled down.

At this time Bibikov, who had twice rolled to the foot of the mountain even before Aufgenapfel, came to and got up on all fours. Then he felt someone falling on him from up above. Bibikov crawled off to the side, turned around, and saw a man lying there in checkered pants. Bibikov sat on a rock and waited.

And the man in checkered pants lay for about four fours without motion, then raised his head and asked into the air: "Whose restaurant is this?"

"What restaurant? This isn't a restaurant," answered Bibikov.

"And who are you?" asked the man in checkered pants.

"I am the mountain climber Bibikov. And who are you?"

"And I am the mountain climber Aufgenapfel."

This is how Bibikov and Aufgenapfel first made one another's acquaintance.

September 1–2, 1936
Translated by Eugene Ostashevsky

The Blue Notebook

FOR THE ALBUM

I once saw a fly and a bedbug get into a fight. It was so frightening that I ran out into the street and ran as far as I could.

The same thing goes for the album: do some dirty thing and then it's too late.

—August 23, 1936

I

My opinion of traveling is succinct: when traveling, do not go too far or else you might see something that will even be impossible to forget. And if anything settles in the memory too stubbornly, a person first starts to feel uneasy, and then it gets quite difficult to keep up the vivacity of the soul.

2

So, for instance: one watchmaker, Comrade Badaev, could not forget a phrase he heard once long ago: "If the sky were crooked, it wouldn't make it any lower." Comrade Badaev didn't really get this saying, it irritated him, he found it unreasonable, even lacking any kind of sense, malignant even, because its claim was obviously incorrect (Comrade Badaev felt that a knowledgeable physicist could say something regarding "the height of the sky" and would question the expression "the sky is crooked." Were this phrase to get to Pearlman, Comrade Badaev was certain, Pearlman would tear its meaning to shreds, the way a young pup tears up house slippers), obviously antagonistic to the normal pattern of European thought. If indeed the claim contained in this saying were true, then it was too unimportant and worthless to speak of. And in any case, hearing this phrase just once, one ought right away to forget it. But he couldn't make that happen: Comrade Badaev constantly remembered this phrase and suffered greatly.

3

It is healthy for a person to know only that which he is supposed to. I can offer the following incident as an example: one person knew a little more, and another a bit less than they were supposed to know. And what happened? The one that knew a bit less got rich, and the one that knew a little more lived his whole life with simply adequate means.

4

Since ancient times, people have wondered about what was smart and what was stupid. In that regard, I remember this incident: when my aunt gave me a writing desk as a gift, I said to myself: "Well now I'll sit down at this desk and the first thought I come up with at this desk will be especially smart." But I could not come up with an especially smart thought. Then I said to myself: "OK, I wasn't able to come up with an especially smart thought, so I'll come up with an especially stupid one." But I couldn't come up with an especially stupid thought either.

5

Everything that's extreme is difficult. The middle parts are done more easily. The very center requires no effort at all. The center is equal to equilibrium. There's no fight in it.

6

Is it necessary to get out of equilibrium?

7

While traveling, do not give yourself over to daydreams, but fantasize and pay attention to everything, even the insignificant details.

8

When sitting in place, do not kick your feet.

9

Any old wisdom is good if somebody has understood it. A wisdom that hasn't been understood may get covered in dust.

10

There lived a redheaded man who had no eyes or ears. He didn't have hair either, so he was called a redhead arbitrarily. He couldn't talk because he had no mouth. He had no nose either. He didn't even have arms or legs. He had no stomach, he had no back, he had no spine, and he had no innards at all. He didn't have anything. So we don't even know whom we're talking about. It's better that we don't talk about him anymore.

—January 7, 1937

11

One grandma had only four teeth in her mouth. Three teeth on top, and one on the bottom. This grandma couldn't chew with these teeth. Truly speaking, they were useless to her. And so grandma decided to pull out all her teeth and insert a corkscrew in her lower gums and minuscule pliers on top. Grandma drank ink, ate beets, and cleaned her ears out with matches. Grandma had four rabbits. Three rabbits on top, and one on the bottom. Grandma used to catch rabbits with her bare hands and put them in little cages. The rabbits cried and scratched their ears with their hind legs. The rabbits drank ink and ate beets. Sha-ha-ha! The rabbits drank ink and ate beets!

12

A certain Pantelei hit Ivan with his heel.

A certain Ivan hit Natalia with a wheel.

A certain Natalia hit Semion with a muzzle.

A certain Semion hit Seliphan with a washbasin.

A certain Seliphan hit Nikita with an overshirt.

A certain Nikita hit Roman with a board.

A certain Roman hit Tatiana with a shovel.

A certain Tatiana hit Elena with a pitcher.

And a fight broke out.

Elena beat Tatiana with a fence.

Tatiana beat Roman with a mattress.

Roman beat Nikita with a suitcase.

Nikita beat Seliphan with a serving tray.
Seliphan beat Semion with his bare hands.
Semion spit into Natalia's ears.
Natalia bit Ivan's fingers.
Ivan kicked Pantelei with his heel.
Ach, we thought, good people fighting each other.

13

One little girl said: "gvya."
Another little girl said: "hphy."
A third little girl said: "mbryu."
And Yermakov chomped, chomped, chomped on cabbages
    under the fence.
Meanwhile, evening was already setting in.
Mot'ka got tired playing in shit and went to bed.
It was drizzling rain.
The swine ate peas.
Rogozin was peeking into the women's bathhouse.
Sen'ka sat on Man'ka in riding position.
Man'ka, meanwhile, drifted off to sleep.
The sky grew dark. The stars twinkled.
Some rats chewed up a mouse under the floorboards.
Sleep, my little boy, and don't let silly dreams scare you.
Silly dreams come from the stomach.

14

Shave your beard and your whiskers!
You ain't goats, so don't wear beards!
You ain't cats, so don't wiggle your whiskers!
You ain't mushrooms, so don't stand around in your hats!

Hey, ladies!
Trim down your hatsies!
Hey, little beauties!
Trim down your skirtsies!
Come on you, Man'ka Marusina,
Come and sit on Pet'ka Elabonin.
Cut your braids off, little girls.
You ain't zebras, so don't run around with tails on.
Chubby little girls,
Invite us over for the festivities.

15

Lead me on with my eyes blindfolded.
I won't go with my eyes blindfolded.
Untie the blindfold from my eyes and I'll go by myself.
Don't hold me by the arms,
I want to give my arms freedom.
Step aside, stupid spectators,
I'm going to start kicking.
I'll walk down one floorboard and I won't lose my balance,
I'll run across the drainpipe and I won't collapse.
Don't get in my way. You'll be sorry.
Your cowardly eyes are unpleasant to the gods.
Your mouths open at the wrong time.
Your noses don't know vibrating smells.
Eat your soup—that's your business.
Sweep your rooms—that's what the age demands of you.
But take those bandages and stomach straps off me,
I live on salt, and you live on sugar.
I have my own flower gardens and vegetable gardens.
In my garden a goat grazes.

In my trunk lies a fur hat.

Don't get in my way, I stand on my own, and you are only a
quart of smoke to me.

—January 8, 1937

16

Today I wrote nothing. Doesn't matter.

—January 9

17

Dmitri eked out pathetic noises.

Anna was weeping, with her head in a pillow.

Mania cried, too.

18

Fedia, hey Fedia!

What sir?

I'll show you what sir!

Silence.

Fedia, hey Fedia!

What's the matter?

Now you son of a bitch! And you ask what's the matter.

What do you want from me?

D'you see that? What do I want from him! You know what I
could do to you, you scoundrel, for words like that . . . I'm
gonna throw you so hard you'll fly into you know where!

Where?

Into the pot.

Silence.

19

Fedia, hey Fedia!
What now, Auntie, have you lost your mind?
Oooh! Oooh! Say that again, come on!
No, I won't.
Now that's better! Know your place! Or else! Enough!

—*February 23, 1937*

20

I choked on a lamb bone.
I was taken by the arms and brought away from the table.
I lost myself in thought.
A mouse ran by.
Ivan ran after the mouse with a long stick.
A strange old woman watched from a window.
Running by the old woman, Ivan hit her in the face with the
stick.

21

Returning home after my walk,
I suddenly exclaimed: Oh my God!
I've been walking four days in a row!
What will my family think of me now?

22

We've died on the fields of the everyday.
No hope is left to lead the way.
Our dreams of happiness are done—
Poverty has won.

—*April 3, 1937*

23

To have only intelligence and talent is too little. One must also have energy, real interest, clarity of thought, and a sense of obligation.

24

Here I write down the events of the day, for they are incredible. In truth: one of the events is particularly incredible, I will underline it.

(1) Yesterday we had nothing to eat. (2) In the morning I took 10 rubles out of the savings bank, leaving 5 in the passbook, so as not to close the account. (3) Stopped by Zhitkov's place and borrowed 60 rubles. (4) Went home, buying food on the way. (5) The weather is wonderful, spring. (6) Went with Marina to the Buddhist pagoda, taking a bag of sandwiches and a flask of wine mixed with water. (7) On the way back we stopped at the pawnshop and *there we saw a pump organ, a Schiedmayer double-manual, a copy of the philharmonic's. The price was only 900 rubles! But half an hour ago it was sold!* (7a) At Alexander's we saw an excellent pipe. 85 rubles. (8) Went to Zhitkov's. (9) With Zhitkov we found out who bought the pump organ and drove to the address: Pesochnaia 31, Apt. 46, Levinsky. (10) Couldn't buy it off him. (11) Spent the evening at Zhitkov's.

—*April 4*

25

Enough of laziness and doing nothing! Open this notebook every day and write down a minimum of half a page. If you have nothing to write down, then, following Gogol's advice, at least write down that today there's nothing to write. Always write with attention and look on writing as a holiday.

26

[This entry was crossed out in the original.]

27

This is how hunger begins:
In the morning you wake lively,
Then weakness,
Then boredom,
Then comes the loss
Of quick reason's strength,—
Then comes calm,
And then horror.

28

Daydreams will be the end of you.
Your interest in this harsh life
Will vanish like smoke. At that time
The herald of the sky will not descend.

Desires and lusts will wilt and then
Youth's ardent thoughts will pass you by . . .
Abandon them! Leave off your dreams, my friend,
Make free of death your mind.

—October 4, 1937

29. THE DAY

Amphibrach
And a little fish flashes in the river's cool wave,
And a little house stands far far away,

And a barking dog barks at a herd of cows,
And Petrov rides a barrow racing down a hill,
And a little flag flutters on top of the house,
And nourishing grain grows ripe in the field,
And the dust shines like silver on every leaf,
And the flies with a whistle fly everywhere,
And young girls lie in the sun to get warm,
And the bees in the garden buzz over the flowers,
And the geese are diving in shadowy ponds,
And the day passes by in its usual labors.

1936–37
Translated by Matvei Yankelevich

»»» «««

One Man Fell Asleep

One man fell asleep a believer but woke up an atheist.

Luckily, this man kept medical scales in his room, because he was in the habit of weighing himself every morning and every evening. And so, going to sleep the night before, he had weighed himself and had found out he weighed four poods and 21 pounds. But the following morning, waking up an atheist, he weighed himself again and found out that now he weighed only four poods thirteen pounds. "Therefore," he concluded, "my faith weighed approximately eight pounds."

1936–37
Translated by Eugene Ostashevsky

A Magazine Article

Right was the emperor Alexander Vilberdat, when he restricted children and their mothers to special areas partitioned off for them in his cities. Pregnant women were impounded there as well, behind a fence, to protect peaceful citizenry from their disgusting appearance.

The great emperor Alexander Vilberdat understood the essence of children no worse than the Flemish painter Teniers. He knew that children are, at best, cruel and petulant old people. Fondness of children is almost the same thing as fondness of embryos, and fondness of embryos is almost the same thing as fondness of excrement.

It is unreasonable to boast: "I am a good person because I love embryos or because I love to defecate." In the same way, it is unreasonable to boast: "I am a good person because I love children."

The great emperor Alexander Vilberdat immediately vomited whenever he saw a child, but this in no way prevented him from being a good person.

I knew a lady who used to say that she would rather pass the night in a stable, a pigpen, a fox lair—anywhere—than a place reeking of children. Yes, indeed, theirs is the most repulsive, I would go as far as to say the most offensive, odor.

Adults get offended by nothing so much as the sight of children. And so, at the time of the great emperor Alexander Vilberdat, to show a child to an adult was taken to be the highest possible affront. It topped spitting into someone's face; and even, say, hitting the inside of the nostril in the process. A "disgrace by child" could be washed off only in a duel, by blood.

1936–38
Translated by Eugene Ostashevsky

》》》　《《《

A Man Once Walked
Out of His House

A man once walked out of his house
With a walking stick and a sack,
    And on he went,
    And on he went:
He never did turn back.

He walked as far as he could see:
He saw what lay ahead.
    He never drank,
    He never slept,
Nor slept nor drank nor ate.

Then once upon a morning
He entered a dark wood
    And on that day,
    And on that day
He disappeared for good.

If anywhere by any chance
You meet him in his travels,
    Then hurry please,
    Then hurry please,
Then hurry please and tell us.

1937
Translated by Matvei Yankelevich and Eugene Ostashevsky

How I Was Visited by Messengers

There was a knocking noise in the clock and the messengers came to me. I did not understand right away that the messengers had come. First, I thought something had gone wrong in the clock. But then I saw that the clock continued ticking and, in all probability, showed the right time. Then I thought that there was a draft in the room. And suddenly I wondered: what kind of phenomenon can this be, for which both the flawed ticking of the clock and a draft in the room can serve as the cause? Thinking this over, I sat in the chair next to the sofa and gazed at the clock. The minute hand stood at nine, and the hour hand near four, therefore it was a quarter to four. Under the clock hung a tear-off calendar, and the calendar's pages fluttered as if a strong wind were blowing in the room. My heart pounded and I was afraid I would lose consciousness.

"I've got to drink some water," I said. On the table next to me stood a pitcher of water. I reached out my hand and took the pitcher.

"Water might help," I said and looked at the water.

It was then I realized that the messengers had come to me, but I could not distinguish them from the water. I was afraid to drink the water, because I might by accident drink up a messenger. What does this mean? This doesn't mean anything. One can drink only liquid. And are messengers liquid? Therefore I could drink the water, there was nothing to fear. But I could not find the water. I walked about the room, looking for it. I tried sticking a belt in my mouth, but it wasn't water. I stuck the calendar in my mouth—this also wasn't water. I forgot about the water and began looking for the messengers. But how is one to find them? What do they look like? I recalled that I could not distinguish them from water, so that meant they must look like water. But what does water look like? I stood and thought.

I don't know how long I stood there and thought, but suddenly I quivered.

"Here's the water!" I said to myself. But it wasn't water, it was only my ear itching.

I started groping under the wardrobe and under the bed, thinking that there I surely would find water or a messenger. But under the wardrobe, among the dust, I found only a ball chewed through by a dog, and under the bed some pieces of broken glass.

Under the chair, I found a partly eaten meatball. I ate it and felt better. The wind was already almost not blowing, and the clock ticked calmly, showing the correct time: a quarter to four.

"Well, so the messengers have already gone," I said to myself and started to change clothes in order to go visit some friends.

August 22, 1937
Translated by Matvei Yankelevich

» » »   « « «

Passacaglia 1

The quiet water swayed at my feet. I stared into the dark water and saw the sky.

Here, at this very spot, Ligudim will tell me the formula for the construction of nonexistent objects.

I will wait until five o'clock, and if Ligudim does not appear among those trees by then, I will leave. I am beginning to feel insulted. I've been standing here for two and a half hours already and the quiet water sways at my feet.

I stuck a stick in the water. Suddenly someone under the water grabbed my stick and jerked on it. I let it out of my hands. The wooden stick disappeared into the water so fast that it even whistled.

I stood by the water and felt frightened and perplexed.

Ligudim arrived exactly at five. It was exactly at five because just then a train sped by across the river: every day exactly at five it flies by that little house.

Ligudim asked me why I looked pale. I told him. Four minutes passed, which Ligudim spent staring into the dark water. Then he said, "This has no formula. You can frighten children with such things but to us it is of no interest. We are not collectors of the fantastic. Only meaningless actions please our hearts. We detest folk art and Hoffmann. A palisade stands between us and mysterious events like these."

Ligudim turned his head in all directions and backed out of my field of vision.

November 10, 1937
Translated by Eugene Ostashevsky and Matvei Yankelevich

Maltonius Olbren

The Plot: M. wishes to rise three feet above the ground. He stands for hours facing the wardrobe. Over the wardrobe hangs a painting, but he can't see it: the wardrobe's in the way. Days, weeks, and months go by. Every day the man stands in front of the wardrobe and tries to rise up into the air. He fails to rise, but he does start to have visions, the same vision every time. Every time he picks out more and more details. M. forgets that he wanted to rise above the ground and gives himself over completely to the study of the vision. And then one time when the maid was cleaning the room, she asked him to take down the painting so that she could wipe the dust off. When M. got up on a stool and glanced at the painting, he saw that the painting depicted what he had seen in his vision. That's when he understood that for a long time already he had been rising into the air, hovering in front of the wardrobe and seeing the painting.

Treatment.

November 16, 1937
Translated by Matvei Yankelevich

»»»   «««

The Four-Legged Crow

There once lived a four-legged crow. Properly speaking, it had five legs, but this isn't worth talking about.

So once this four-legged crow bought itself some coffee and thought, "OK, so I bought coffee, what I am supposed to do with it now?"

Just then, unfortunately, a fox was running by. The fox saw the crow and shouted. "Hey," it shouted, "you crow!"

And the crow shouted back: "Crow yourself!"

And the fox shouted to the crow: "You're a pig, crow, that's what you are!"

The crow was so insulted it scattered the coffee. And the fox ran off. And the crow climbed down and went on its four, or to be more precise, five legs to its lousy house.

February 13, 1938
Translated by Eugene Ostashevsky

The Adventure of Katerpillar

Mishurin was a katerpillar. For this reason, or maybe not for this reason, he liked to lie under the sofa or behind the wardrobe and suck dust. Since he wasn't an especially neat man, sometimes for the entire day his mug was covered with dust like with down.

Once he received an invitation to someone's house, and Mishurin decided to rinse his face a bit. He poured warm water into the basin, spritzed in a little vinegar, and submerged his face in this water. Apparently, there was too much vinegar in the water, and so Mishurin went blind. Until extreme old age he got around by touch, and for this reason, or maybe not for this reason, began to resemble a katerpillar even more.

October 16, 1940
Translated by Eugene Ostashevsky

Nikolai Zabolotsky

The Signs of the Zodiac Go Dark

The signs of the Zodiac go dark
Above the free space of the fields.
The Dog animal sleeps,
The Sparrow bird snoozes.
Ample-bottomed mermaids
Rise into the sky,
With arms hard as sticks,
With breasts spherical as turnips.
A witch that lands on a triangle
Turns into smoke.
A cadaver does the cakewalk
With two rustic Russian dryads.
In the back the pale chorus
Of necromancers hunts the Fly
And above the forest
The moon glows, motionless and high.

The signs of the Zodiac go dark
Over village cottages.
The Dog animal sleeps,
The Flounder fish snoozes.
The rattle murmurs knock-knock-knock,
The Spider animal sleeps,
The Cow sleeps, the Fly sleeps,

Over the earth hangs the moon.
Over the earth hangs a large bowl
Of overturned water.
A log emerges from the ruffled
Beard of a local troll.
A siren shows the comely span
Of leg from under a little cloud,
Slurping, a cannibal devours
What made the gentleman a man.
All mix in the common dance
And everywhere hop and traipse
Fleas, cadavers, witches, wenches,
British lords and brutish apes.

Graduate of centuries gone,
General of a novel era,
My reason! These monsters
Are only fantasy and fiction.
Only fantasy, delirium,
Rocking of a drowsy thought,
Inconsolable suffering—
Things that are not . . .

High up is the terrestrial haven.
It is late. It's time to sleep.
Reason, my poor warrior,
Curl up silent in your crib.
Lay aside your doubts, worries.
The day has passed and you and I—
Half-beasts, half-gods—
Fall asleep upon the threshold
Of the new life of labor.

The rattle murmurs knock-knock-knock,
The Spider animal sleeps,
The Cow sleeps, the Fly sleeps,
Over the earth hangs the moon.
Over the earth hangs a large bowl
Of overturned water.
The Potato vegetable sleeps.
Fall asleep now. Bye-bye.

1929
Translated by Eugene Ostashevsky

The Temptation

Death comes to the man,
Says, "Hey, boss,
You look like an invalid
Bitten by insects.
Leave your living, come with me,
My coffin is peaceful.
I shroud in white linen
Everyone, young and old.
Don't grieve you're headed for the pit,
And that's the end of your learning.
The field will plow itself,
The rye will ripen unreaped.
The sun will be hot at noon,
Cooler toward evening.
Whereas you will sleep
The sleep of the experienced,
Beneath a square bronze cross
In a clean coffin."

"Hands off, Death,"
Replies the peasant.
"Have mercy on me,
Old age is already unpleasant.
Grant me a small reprieve,

Do me that favor
And I'll give you my only daughter
In reward for your labor."

Death does not weep does not laugh:
It takes the maiden in its arms
And runs like a tongue of flame
Over the bending grass
Along the garden path.

In the field there's a mound,
In the mound the maid makes moan:
"It's hard lying in the coffin,
Both of my arms have turned black,
My hair became as dust,
Feather grass sprouts from my breasts.
It's hard lying in the grave,
My thin lips have rotted,
My eye sockets are empty,
I have no boyfriend."

Death flies over the mound,
Laughs hysterically and weeps,
Shoots at it from a rifle,
And says, bending down:
"OK, baby, enough chatter,
The grave's no place for yadda-yadda!
A world exists above the world,
Lay aside the coffin board!
Hark, the wind blows in the field,
Evening settles on the grass.
Caravans of sleepy stars
Hurriedly flew over us.

Quit your underground fast,
Try and rise! What's past is past."

The maiden stirs her arm,
First slowly, as if in a dream,
Then knocks the board out, jumps out,
And—splat!—bursts along the seams.

And the poor girl streams, streams
In the manner of intestines.
Where her camisole once was,
What is there now? Only dust.
Blushing maggots show their faces
From her corporeal orifices:
Sucking in the pinkish liquid
They resemble swaddled infants.
She used to be a maiden, now she's slop.
Laughter, don't laugh, stop!
The loam will crack when the sun will rise,
Right away will the maiden rise.

From her shinbone
A tree will grow,
The tree will rustle,
Sing songs about the maiden,
Sing songs about the maiden,
Ring out with its sweet voice:
"Lulla, lulla, lullaby,
Lullaby my baby girl!
The wind blew into the dale,
The crescent in the sky went pale,
Peasants sleep in their huts,
Each has many many cats.

And every pretty kitty–cat
Has a red gate,
They wear blue fur coats,
They walk in gold boots,
They walk in gold boots,
Very, very expensive boots . . ."

1929
Translated by Eugene Ostashevsky

The Triumph of Agriculture

[*selections*]

PROLOGUE

Not very nice, although good-looking,
Who's that staring at us?
It's a deliberate peasant
Directing his eyes through his glasses.
Departments of white granaries
Rose in the distance,
Bread looked out of the window,
A horse stood behind a partition.
Nature was lying everywhere
In a horrible wild mess:
A tree rocked to and fro,
The tress of a river hardly flowed.
Two or three huts
Slouched over an insane brook.
One evening there walks by
An elliptical bear.
And above him a crane,
Big and ugly,
Flies around whooping
And shaking its head in the silent sky.

From its beak there hangs a scroll,
Which says: "Three-crop tillage
Is unprofitable."
The peasant strokes the end of his beard.

2. THE SUFFERINGS OF ANIMALS

The uncertain bodies of animals
Sat, crowded together in a shed.
They spoke to one another freely,
They spoke the language of nature.
"I hardly know myself,"
Said the bull, looking into the window.
"I bear the stamp of consciousness
And it has made me old at heart.
What am I to do with my doubt?
How do I silence my worry?
It would seem that the day is done
Without incident, and good riddance!
But it isn't that simple.
I bend under the yoke of depression.
Soon, soon I will be thrown
To the bottom of a bovine cemetery.
O moan funereal,
Doleful lamentation!
How horrible these words are: 'mass grave'!
A dead cow lies there in a heap
Over a sheep's crushed bones
As, to the side, a dog takes out its anger
By mutilating a corpse.
Somewhere a decomposing hoof
Provides a plant with nutrient;

That catalyst of putrefaction, worm
Has in a loose skull made his home;
Pieces of skin and contents of an eye socket
Lie here, altogether scrambled,
And, condensing in the thicket,
Only the dewdrops glisten and tremble."

The horse replied:
"It's the masses that squint, wishing to read
Death's illegible creed—
Can't you tell need from need?
We need to know the bitter root of life.
In my elliptical skull
The brain lies like an oblong aspic
But it's not some dumb drone
Yawning in its slanting home.
Humans! In vain do you think
That I don't know how to think,
Since you beat me with a stick,
Since you shove the bit in my mouth.
The peasant hugs me with his knees
And hops, aggressively wielding a whip,
And, my eyes bugged out, I gallop
Grabbing the air with a greedy mouth.
Nature around me collapses,
The crippled world rocks to and fro,
Weeping, the flowers die
Because I knock them over with my feet.
A daisy, feeling the blow,
Closes her eyes and hits the sod
As on my back
The peasant like a horrible god

Waves around his arms and legs.
But when I stand there in my stall,
Dispirited and winded,
Like an apartment window
I open up my consciousness.
And then, by pain deformed, I hear
The howling of the heavenly spheres:
It is some animal bewailing his sentence
To rotate the machine called 'wheel.'
Must it be so? I beg you, friends,
Are we but means for human ends?"

The horse fell silent. Everyone paused
In the grasp of primitive consciousness.
The composite body of animals
Looked like a poor corpse.
A lamp pumped full of kerosene
Swung burning like a martyr,
The light it cast so trembling and ancient
That being and nonbeing seemed as one.
Memories, the glum
Children of suffering,
Crowded together in the minds
Of the persistent animals.
And into two the double world split,
Its drop cloth tearing to reveal
An emptiness, cerulean and infinite.

"I have a vision of a cheerless graveyard,"
The bull said with burning eyes.
"There, on a sloping hillside
Someone sleeps at the bottom of a damp grave.
Who is he, pitiful, all in scabs,

Forgotten and half-eaten,
This inhabitant of a poor cemetery,
Dressed in an unkempt nimbus?
Nights languish around him
Resting on pale arms,
Flowers mutter around him
In funereal gossamer.
And, invisible to men
But gnarled and muscular like oak trees,
Rise the intelligent witnesses of his life—
The Tables of Destiny.
And everybody reads with stately eyes
The inventions of the interesting corpse
That reconcile the world of animals
Foolishly-beautifully with the skies.
Centuries will pass and pass,
Our children's children will be aged,
But even they will find peace
At the shore of such a grave.
Thus a man, fallen out of his time
And buried in the mire of Novgorod,
Has sown in the soul of nature
The beautiful image of man."

None spoke. None dared to believe.
Big-lipped, the horse was lost in daydreams.
And the night danced, like the first night,
Like a roman candle on the roof,
Till suddenly it fell. The light
Burst forth and the majestic sphere
Rose. And, witnesses of words spoke in the night,
The birds sang out in the air.

3. THE KULAK, RULER OF FARM LABORERS

Birds, witnesses of words spoke in the night,
Sang out in the air,
As constellations cast
Primeval light on the high grass.
Above the sublime village
The Russian moon rose
Still obscure and perverse,
Again in her ancient crown.

Massing in heavy chests
His coins with heads of kings,
The kulak nestled among people.
He experienced perpetual fear.
Next to him nestled his gods
In their pensive god-frames.
Disheveled, feeble, bipedal,
In crowns, armor, hair shirts,
With large extraordinary beards,
They looked out from behind the glass
To where the kulak, crossing himself with his hands,
Cracked slow bows.
The kulak carries out his prayers.
A dog is barking. Parca stands guard.
And Time extemporizes
Down, down the incline of a shore.
Nature drools with juice,
The vegetables are full of silence.
Lazily grows the cereal,
Short, feeble, blind.
The earth, in need of crude salt,

Shouts to him, "Hey, kulak, halt!"
But it can threaten all it wants,
The kulak will destroy the harvest.
He finds pleasure in erasure
Of the signs of the future
And all the cereals infirm
Stand, hardly suppressing their yawns.

The kulak, ruler of farm laborers,
Sat on mountains of pelf
And his egocentric universe
Above some clouds set itself.
Just then the night, rustling its wings,
Runs on the rooftop like a witch,
She sometimes sends the wind into the fields,
She sometimes hides and holds her breath,
She sometimes tears the shutter from the window
And shouts, "Get up, you damn crow!
A tornado rides over the world,
Go for it, grasp it with your hands,
Set up barbed-wire entanglements,
Or else you will die
And lie around unmoving with your guts out!
Through battles, through thunder, through labor
I see the flow of big water,
I see the Dnieper sewed up in concrete,
I see the Caucasus in electric lights,
The steel horse bearing corn,
The iron ox bearing malt liquor.
Levers of plows, spears of harrows
Upturn the soil of centuries

And you got a lot to answer for
Before the earth, you old crow!"
The kulak wails on a bench,
Scratches his black sides with nails,
And the dog barks, filled with foreboding,
At a many-legged crowd.
You could hear the soldier speak
And the door creak, and in an hour
One bearded figure
Had already left us.
This universal exile, this miser
Sat taking in the jingle of the bells,
He bade his hut good-bye in thought,
He rocked in the cart like a drunk.
And night, the builder of the day,
With fortitude and courage
Flew off the roof like a witch
As the cart bore down into the abyss.

5 · THE DAWN OF SCIENCE

When the midnight bird
Solemnly flew in the grasses,
The pensive faces of peasants
Shone after the tempest.
Above the world of grief and pain
Rang out the clarinet of the swain
And when he sang his shepherd's song
The cows' choir sang along
To the life-giving sphere that took
Position over oak and brook.

Praise to the world, peace to the earth,
War to the rich and the kings of the land!
The morning's many-fingered hand
Holds the red atom of rebirth.
The red atom of rebirth,
Fiery lamp of millions,
Its movement over the earth
Colors it vermilion.
People rose and the cows rose,
The horses rose and oxen.
Here a soldier comes. He's crimson
From his head down to his boot.
In the midst of a large herd
Is he a demon or a god?
The winged star upon his crest
Faces in the direction of the east.

SOLDIER:

O cows, I had a dream.
I slept, wrapped up in sheepskins,
And the skies opened to reveal
A large animal institute.
There life was always full of health.
At the center of the edifice
A stately cow stood in the wreath
Of incomplete consciousness.
Goddess of cheese, goddess of milk,
Touching the ceiling with her head,
She modestly covered herself with a nightshirt
And squeezed her breasts into a barrel.
With loud banging, ten thick streams
Fell on the cold metal,

And, readied for commercial freight,
The pail sounded like music,
As the enthusiastic cow,
Pressing her hands to her chest,
Stood there, ready for the challenge
Of raising her consciousness.

COWS:

It's strange to hear such speeches,
Knowing the thoughts of men.
Tell us, what happened later?
What did the others do?

SOLDIER:

I saw a red glow in the window
Belonging to a rational ox.
The parliament of ponderous cows
Sat there engaged in problem solving.
A donkey, giggling like a goose,
Showed signs of having a screw loose.
He laughed at them but like an opus
In species similar to grass
Vegetable reason grew unfocused
In his animalistic head.
That donkey dug the dry mountain sod
For cast-iron potatoes,
But down below the temple of machinery
Manufactured oxygen pancakes.
There horses, friends of chemistry,
Ate polymeric soup,
Some others sailed in midair
Expecting visitors from the sky.
A cow in formulas and ribbons

Baked pie out of elements
And large chemical oats
Grew in protective coats.

HORSE:

What an astounding country,
So full of science and fun!
I listen to your stories
As if imbibing wine.
I feel strangely light-headed.
I bet there's sweat on my brow.
Young soldier, you're putting us on,
No more blue-collar toil at the plow?
Now it's our reason you need,
Not our sinewy meat?
Listen, I am old and tired.
After a lifetime of push and pull
I should be honorably retired
And you want me to go to chemistry school? Ha!

SOLDIER:

Get off your high horse, silly palfrey,
Don't interrupt my narrative!
Your waggish jokes aren't worth a paltry
Cigarette butt! Don't be so negative!
My mind is like yours, no more
Than a pot full of sawdust,
But rise against your nature. Trust
This beautiful tableau . . .
Above the Equine Institute
The moon was shining full of beauty.
The dishes lay in scientific desuetude,
The spindle offered rest conjoined with duty.

The donkey enters. He is hungry.
He limps and leans upon a comrade.
They ply him like a babe with nourishment
And aid his mental development.
Here butterflies are trained in labor
And garden snakes learn science:
How to manufacture thread and mica,
How to sew gloves and pants.
Here the wolf sings the evening star
With an iron microscope,
Here a horse engages in parley
With radishes and parsley.
And the harmonious choirs of men
Abandoning the pastures of ether
Descend onto the haystacks of the world
To taste the food of swans.

HORSE:

Are you done?

SOLDIER:

I am done.

HORSE:

Bravo, bravo!
This fellow has more lies than a library!
But sweet is the poison you speak,
And your damn ravings eat at my heart.
Soldier! We go naked and barefoot.
Plows crush us, bees sting us,
Our minds are like huts in the slum,
Our tails drag through the dust.
Soldier, during your midnight vigils,
In the smoke of the autumn evening,

Haven't you ever heard an ox
Fighting for breath in your heavy stocks?
We have no rights before the law,
The plow calls us and next the grave.
Death is the only state we know
That welcomes us as refugees.

SOLDIER:

Shame, horsey! What's come over you?
You hardly know what you are saying.
Look, what is that thundering thing
That crawls from out behind the mountain to replace you?
Huge, two-storied, made of iron,
With an iron mug in flames,
He crawls toward us, thundering. He is
Indefatigable as warrior against nature
And fights her in the field hand to hand.
So—courage, O intelligent cows,
Courage, O horses, bulls, courage!
From now on you'll be healthy, fit.
We'll build you shelters here with heaping
Platters of assorted feed.
We'll crush the monarchy of plows,
We'll raze the old world to the ground,
And for the first time the letter *A*
We'll say together and very loud.

The far-off forest roared
A dull roll of the letter *A*
As, clanging, the tractor crawled out
Smashing through centuries with its face.
And the crowds of feeble animals,

Fallen into dust and ash,
Looked up with dry primeval eyes
At the new face of the earth.

1929–30
Translated by Eugene Ostashevsky

The Battle of Elephants

Listen, warrior of words:
Let the night sing with your swords!

The horses of adjectives trample
The faltering figures of nouns,
Shaggy horsemen put to flight
The cavalry of verbs,
And shells of interjections
Burst overhead
Like flares.

Battle of words! Combat of senses!
There's general ruckus in the tower of Syntax!
The Europe of consciousness feels the fraction
Of insurrection.
Into the mouths of enemy cannons
Firing with smashed letters
The war elephants of the subconscious
Crawl out and shuffle
Like giant dwarfs.

They haven't eaten since birth, these creatures.
They dash into the mysterious breaches
And rear in glee
As human figures dangle from their mouths pathetically.

Elephants of the subconscious!
War beasts of the underworld!
They stand and greet with joyful squealing
This chaos of rioting, this orgy of stealing!

Little elephant eyes
Fill with laughter and joy.
So many toys! And the petards so loud!
Cannons fall silent after dining on blood,
Syntax builds houses totally dotty,
The world stands in awkward beauty.
The old arboreal dispensation is reversed,
The battle has given the trees a new earth.
They converse, they write essays, they swing,
The whole world is filled with awkward meaning!
A wolf put on a human face
In place of a broken snout,
Took out his flute and sounds the wordless, irreverent
First song of the war elephants!

Poetry's crown is torn.
She lost the battle.
The Alps of ancient towers have collapsed
Where numbers shone on nave and apse,
Where the sword of syllogism glinted acutely
Attested by pure reason.
And what for? It lost the battle
To babble of another mettle.

Poetry, in spiritual pain,
Cries "All is vain!
All has gone down the drain!"
Disdains the world,

Wants to commit seppuku
And sometimes laughs like one insane,
And sometimes flees into the corn
And sometimes rolls in the dust in spiritual pain.

Really, how could it so befall
That the ancient capital fell?
The whole world was used to poetry,
Everything was so clear.
Cavalry lined up in order,
Painted numbers on cannons,
And on flags the word MIND
Nodded to everyone, like their kin and kind.
And suddenly these elephants arrive
Turning everything upside down!

Poetry starts to pay attention,
To study the movements of the new figures,
The beauty of awkwardness dawns on her,
The beauty of an elephant thrown up by the underworld.

The war has ended. In the dust
Vegetables writhe in vernal lust.
And the elephant, being tamed by rationality,
Eats pies and drinks them down with tea.

1931
Translated by Eugene Ostashevsky

The Test of the Will

AGAFONOV:

    Please sit down, have some tea.

    We have preserves in every pot.

KORNEEV:

    Among the dishes I distinguish

    The English teapot.

AGAFONOV:

    Your eye, Korneev, has grown sharp,

    You see the porcelain of England.

    It has appeared in our cell

    Since not so very long ago.

    A friend entrusted it to my care

    Out of a trunk full of tableware.

KORNEEV:

    Your discourse oversteps all measure,

    O Agafonov, my heart's companion,

    I can't believe it. No! This precious

    Object, worthy of Pantheons,

    This specter of luxurious Britain,

    Whose bearing gratifies the eye,

    Instructs the soul, enlightens reason,

    Heals the infirm with art,

    Melts the defenses of the heart,

    While shining forth like a light—

How can it be? This elegant relic,
Redolent of a superior world,
Restores the sage in his monastic dwelling
With water colored by an herb?

AGAFONOV:

Yes, it's true.

KORNEEV:

Good God!
An object of such leverage
Stands, full of poison,
Providing Agafonov with beverage!
To think it only: among handles
That are as graceful as meringue,
It could have subsisted in better conditions:
In state of worship, like an angel.
The sovereign of misty Albion
Would have installed it on a dais,
And sat before it, richly perfumed,
Whispering this dish's praise.
The crown prince, in his very person,
Would enter its presence upon his tiptoes,
Considering it a favor personal
To be allowed to tap its nose.
Instead, what have we here? Fictions!
Fallen into a modest hut,
This teapot offers us refreshment
Although you're not a duke or a count.

AGAFONOV:

Encyclopedias of lies
I've heard from sundry sycophants,
But from you, my friend Korneev,
I expected otherwise.

You judge, I swear, like a lunatic,
By passions woefully distorted.
The little vein upon your forehead
Pulsates with an unseemly tic.
This teapot—can it be the cause?
Then take it. Wherefore I need it?

KORNEEV:

I thank you, sir.
Now I am quite calm.
Farewell. I am still weeping. [*Leaves.*]

AGAFONOV:

My spirit hovers in the air,
My body lies in this cell,
And I invite the teapot back right now.

KORNEEV [*Enters*]:

Take back this teapot, Agafonov.
I shall abhor its sight forever.
I used to be a man of wisdom
But I am ruined now and lost.

AGAFONOV [*Embracing him*]:

Praise be to you, my friend Korneev.
Your spirit has vanquished this teapot!
Now, I beg you, please accept it
As my eager and earnest gift.

1931
Translated by Eugene Ostashevsky

The Poem of Rain

WOLF:

>O honorable forest snake,
>Where do you crawl without knowing
>Where to crawl and why to hurry?
>Is a hurried life worth living?

SNAKE:

>O reverend wolf, the mind finds strange
>That world which is without change.
>Our flight is as elementary
>As that of smoke issuing from a chimney.

WOLF:

>Your answer isn't hard to get.
>Snakes cannot deal in abstract notions.
>It is yourself you flee, my friend,
>Assigning meaning unto motion.

SNAKE:

>I see you're a philosophical idealist!

WOLF:

>Look: a leaf falls from the tree.
>The cuckoo, building its song
>On two tones (what a simple creature!)
>Sings in the high groves.
>A limpid sun-shower comes,
>The water falls for two–three minutes

And barefoot the peasants frolic,
And then it's clear again, the rain
Has ended. Tell me
The meaning of this picture.

SNAKE:

Go talk to wolves. They'll tell you why
Water falls out of the sky.

WOLF:

Excellent. I'll go to the wolves.
Water flows down their sides.
Water sings softly like a mother
When it as softly falls on us.
Nature in a stately dress
With the sun resting on her head
Plays on the organ the whole day.
We call this: life.
We call this: rain,
Splashing of children in puddles,
Sounds of trees, dances of groves
The guffawing of violets.
Or, when the organ sounds glum
The sky reverberates like a drum,
And many tons of storm clouds lie
On every point of the sky,
When mighty torrents' iron fist
Knocks off his feet the forest beast,
With sentiment sinking and odd
We call this: God.

1931
Translated by Eugene Ostashevsky

Time

1

Heracles, Tycho, Leo, and Thomas
Sat majestically in the house.
Above them an ancestral lamp
Shone, shedding light upon the table.
This lamp was luxurious and ancient.
It had the form of a cast-iron woman.
The woman hung down from chains,
Oil was poured in the small of her back
To keep the wick aflame,
To ward off darkness.

2

Around them the decorous
Room shone, prepared for the feast.
By the walls—a well-provisioned chest,
There—the image of an idol
From expensive alabaster.
In the pot flowered a large aster.
And chairs on legs without rottenness
Stood around the walls monotonous.

3

This room was populated with
Four feasting guests.
Sometimes they leaped up,
Grabbed the shanks of their glasses,
And piercingly cried *Vivat!*
A lamp shone at two hundred watts.
Heracles was a forest soldier,
He had a grouse of a rifle,
On that grouse there was a large trigger.
Applying pressure on it with your finger,
You might slay animals in quantity.

4

Heracles spoke like himself,
Depicting a forceful figure:
"I adore women since childhood.
They represent a sumptuous keyboard
From which you can extract eloquent chords."
The muzzles of animals slain in combat
Stared down from the walls.
The clock ticked on.
Unable to contain his active mind,
The pensive Thomas uttered:
"Yes, great is the significance of women,
I do not doubt it
And yet the thought of time is greater. Yes!
Let us sing the ditty about time which we always sing."

5. DITTY ABOUT TIME

Silent, the stream from goblet *A*
Flows into goblet *B*.
A maid makes lace.
Stars dance on the chimney.

Andromeda and Equuleus
Swung to face the north,
Packs of astral flames
Rose above the earth.

Year by year, day by day,
We burn up with astral flame,
Children of constellations, cry,
Extend our arms to Andromeda

And leave forever having seen
How soundlessly
The stream from goblet *A*
Flows into goblet *B*.

6

And then the glasses rang again
And everybody cried *Vivat!* unanimously
And in response to their din
The clock produced five shouts glamorously.
As if it were a small cathedral
That firmly hangs down from a nail,
From long ago the clock cried out
Directing stars in their sail.
O bottomless chest of time,
O handiwork of hell, O clock!

And, perfectly understanding all this,
Said Thomas, aiding thought in its birth:
"I do propose we extirpate the clock!"
Then he gave his mustache a twirl
And looked at everyone in pensive calmness.
The woman shone with her cast-iron pelvis.

7

Had they looked out of the window
They would have witnessed the great spot
Of the evening luminary.
There vegetables grew like flutes,
Flowers swayed higher than shoulders,
And through each grass-blade, like through the stomach
    lining,
The light could flow.
A city of meaty plants traversed
The stream of water.
And the long naked leaves
Applauded with their bodies,
And the lower sinews bathed
In the chemical water.

8

After he stared through the window with disgust,
Said Thomas: "Nor cranberry, nor loganberry,
Nor beetle, mill, or birdie,
Nor the large buttock of woman
Rejoice me. By your leave:
The clock ticks on, and I will leave."

9

Then the silent Leo rises,
Savagely picks up the rifle,
Inserts two bullets in the barrel,
Pours the fatal powder
And at the center of the clockface
Shoots with all his power.
They stand there like gods in smoke
And whisper terribly, *Vivat!*
As the legs of the iron woman
Burn over them at two hundred watts.
And all the vegetables press
Against the gluelike glass
And stare astounded upon
The grave of human reason.

1933
Translated by Eugene Ostashevsky

Nikolai Oleinikov

In Service of Science

I described the grasshopper, I described the bee,
I depicted birds from their best angles,
But how can I describe the gleam
Of hairs on your head that lie untangled?

Alas, I do not have that erstwhile power
That, similar to death, mowed down ladies in full flower!
I'm not what I once was. My madness is extinct, my fire
　　spent.
I cannot stomach former nourishment.

Ducks do not pass in shape of dinner
Through my dilapidated innards.
I do not let love's suffering take its course—
I am attracted to the framework of the universe.

Millet calls me to ponder,
Tooth powders move me and inspire me to think,
I magnify a butterfly with a magnifying glass—
I find its structure very interesting.

I am pursued through offices and boulevards
By secret fantasies of turpentine,
By dreams of matches, thoughts of bedbugs,
Of sundry knickknacks, practical and handy,

What are the hidden mechanisms of beetles,
What is the force that acts inside a candy.

I understood croissants
And wherefore men submerge mushrooms in brine,
The pregnant sense of horse-drawn sleighs and carts,
Why windows are reflected in cows' eyen,
Though what's the use of windows to a bovine?

Love dissipates and passion lies.
                              Yet there it is, beyond reproach,
The marvelous structure of the cockroach.
O energetic cockroachy legs, whose number equals six,
They're saying something, they're scribbling on air,
Their forms are full of secret meaning. . . .
                    Yes, in the cockroach, there's something there,
When its whiskers flutter and its paws make little kicks.

But where are the ladies, you will ask, where are the dear
    girlfriends
That shared with me my nightly fandango,
Recalling tubs and decanters with their curves and bends,
Where do they go?

Some are no more. The others, far away.
They all burned up like candles, I would say,
And I burn with a different fire and a different mission:
I'm on a mission to outperform my competition.
I heed the call to great new achievements
Proposed by congresses of forest grass each evening.
There, beetles pass their time in interesting debate,
A grasshopper cycles by—he's worried—he's late!—
A tiny bug is baffled by a marigold
And circles its corona.

It runs and runs . . . I notice this agility and sadness takes
    hold,
My heart sinks with an "Oh no!"
I remember the days when in freshness I exceeded a horse
    (or was at least akin)
And feel the gnawing of a secret vitamin.
I tense my hands in silence,
I stare at grass without any fun.
Yet hark!—'Tis what?—The tympanum! And the
    unhurried sun
Rises above the hierophant of science.

1932
Translated by Eugene Ostashevsky

Gluttony: A Ballad

The first time I saw you
I admired your face,
The second time I saw you,
You lay in my embrace.

Our one-hundredth meeting
I turned distant and cold.
Then unto you
My heart I told:

"I cannot love you
Without butter and bread.
To salvage our passion
Bake pie instead.

Look how I wither
From day unto day.
Tatiana, Tatiana,
Feed me, I say!

Feed me and serve me
Excellent food.
Boil *pelmeni,*
Ham also is good.

When I'm on fire
With potato and pea,
I'll love you gently,
Beautifully, eagerly . . .
Feed me!"

Tatiana stands up
And goes to the kitchen.
She comes back with a pickle,
She comes back with chicken.

Quickly the body
Recovered its force.
Again my deeds took
The unnamable course.

Again some more chicken,
Again some more love.
What great harm to my body
Was I capable of!

It was light outside
When I quieted myself.
Under the windows
A drunk called for help.

I lay in deep sleep
For three nights and three days.
My bones like the sea
Creaked with malaise.

When I woke up,
Soft was my moan.
Then terror pierced
Me down to the last bone.

I'm grabbing my leg
But the leg doesn't run.
I'm squeezing my heart
But the heart doesn't thump.

. . . And then I die.

At a cemetery
Buried I lie.
Beneath a horseblanket
I shake and I cry.

I'm crying because
Of decomposition:
I'm twice as hungry
In that condition.

Who'll supply me with food,
All kinds of meat,
Beautiful tea,
Beautiful sweets?

I don't want any love,
Passion, avaunt!
It's lemonade
And tomatoes I want.

Nobody comes.
The coffin board creaks
And the heart of a poet
Despairingly ticks.

This heart will soon
Fall silent and wither

And yellow water
Spurt out thither.

The world will keep turning,
Eternally fresh,
As a pink blind worm
Feels its way through my flesh.

October 1932
Translated by Eugene Ostashevsky

》》》 《《《

To a Lady Unwilling to Renounce Consumption of Meat from Cherkassy

Madam, avoid beef.
It brings your stomach wall to grief.
It lays its seal onto your intestine.
Eating it will make you squeal from strife internecine.

Not so with rabbits. Their caloric play
Recalls a sunny summer day.

1932
Translated by Eugene Ostashevsky

An Epistle to a Theatrical Actress

Miss, I saw you yesterday
First in clothing, then without.
The sensation was, no doubt,
Greater than I can convey.

Above the cardiovascular system
Branching out like a bush,
Swifter than a flock of sparrows
My emotions made a whoosh.

No, I swear, this is not
Hatred, poisonous to blood.
It is love, unhappy love,
I'll take it with me to my grave.

I also harbor other feelings,
That go under the name of "desire."
Lisa! You're my favorite artist!
Let me cleave to you and expire!

1932
Translated by Eugene Ostashevsky

For the Recovery of Heinrich

Good-bye, asceticism. Let us praise
The egg, whose yolk from center never strays.
Let us praise chicken, and its bitter liver,
And pickles, out of the hardiest barrels delivered!

The marvelous word "bottle"
Upon me does its work.
Napkin, pepper shaker, fork—
All words whose meaning has no bottom.

I am astounded by the sound of glasses,
The brilliant play of vodka, refracting light,
In honor of Heinrich, who all bons vivants surpasses,
I propose to drink tonight.

Let us get soused, friends! What else can be
The happy outcome of his recovery?

Let his soul taste—it won't be disappointed—
The vivifying mix of vinegar and mustard.
I hope his legs, his muscles, and his joints
Regain their former force and bluster.

Just one last toast to Heinrich, his inextinguishable passion
For all things that were dear to his heart,

The round breast and movement delicate,
Luxurious, full shoulders and the legs' extension.

But he must not combine chicken thighs with shameless
    female thighs,
He must not mix passion and protein!
My dear Heinrich! I am sorry. Your cuisine
(By which I mean "routine") prohibits spice.

There is a time and a measure for all things.
Tobacco is for cigarettes, and for matches, sulfur.
Desire may well be what women are for
But only the lentil satiation brings.

1932
Translated by Eugene Ostashevsky

Charles Darwin

Charles Darwin, the noted biologist,
Took a titmouse into his grasp.
He observed it with great attention,
Its beauty was making him gasp.

He studied its serpentine forehead,
Its scaly and cloven fishtail,
The paws that resembled the Pleiades,
The mousy lean in its sail.

"I must say," considered Charles Darwin,
"I must say that the creature's complex.
Compared to it I am nobody.
Just a birdie—but look at those pecs!

Why, why was Nature so cruel
To me when she doled out her pie?
Why did I get these ugly cheeks,
These banal heels, this chest like a wheel—why?"

The old man burst into tears,
He took out his pistol and ball.
Charles Darwin was a famous biologist,
But he wasn't good-looking at all.

1933
Translated by Eugene Ostashevsky

The Fly

I was madly in love with a fly.
O friends, it was so long ago,
When I was happy and young,
When young and happy was I.

I would pick up a microscope,
Observing her studiously:
Her cheeks, her eyes, and her forehead—
And then I'd direct it at me!

And I saw that the two of us
Were complementary to no end,
That she was in love with me too,
My glittering, many-legged girlfriend.

She flew in circles above me,
She knocked and she beat on the glass.
Sometimes we would join in a kiss.
What was time to me when she loved me?

But years have passed and disease
Holds me with oppressive caress.
In my ears, in my back, in my knees,
Shooting pains interrupt my rest.

I now am no longer myself
And my fly, oh, my fly is no more.
She no longer buzzes and sings,
She no longer knocks on the window.

An invisible serpent doth gnaw at my heart
And forgotten emotions are stirred.
There's nothing before me now, nothing . . .
O my fly! O my trembling bird!

1934
Translated by Eugene Ostashevsky

Zeros

The sight of a notebook is pleasant,
There a powerful zero is present,
And another, but smaller and crippled,
Like a lemon lies nearby, rippled.

My dear, my dear zeros,
I loved you and I love you still.
Be quick, melancholics! Hurry, depressives!
Rub a zero and all will be well.

These circles are wonderfully curative,
Each one worth a doctor or nurse:
With them, the patient thinks positive,
Without them, he cries for a hearse—or worse!

When I go, do not crown my tombstone
With an expensive, impractical wreath.
Rather lay with your trembling fingers
A zero upon the heath.

1934?
Translated by Eugene Ostashevsky

Leonid Lipavsky

Water Tractatus

When in a restaurant, you involuntarily think of space.

The champion took a steel wire and ran an apple straight through.

"Here is a world," he said, "which has no name. It lies under the lowest border of human language. It is one of the worlds that never made it."

"And yet it has its own shape, its own forms," said the captain. "Its life evidently consists of them. This is a marvelous world, you can pray to it if you want. . . . Or do they have no meaning? No, I don't believe that."

"Why not avoid these intricacies? Shouldn't it suffice to pass from one piece of glass to another?" asked the diminutive Greek. "Through yellow glass all things will recall the tender section of an orange. And what if the pieces change their color every hour, like the spectrum? I shall live in a multicolored gazebo, carefree like a landlord."

"They can change their angle of refraction," said the captain.

"I understand this," said the fourth speaker. "We are separated by time and space—totally and forever. Yet we burn with mad curiosity. We wish to be all objects and beings, to be temperature, wave, transformation. An unquenchable thirst for encounter will not let me alone."

Then the champion stood up and raised his glass:

"I drink to the tropical sensation."

"What tropical sensation?"

THE CHAMPION'S TALE

You walk on a hot day along a meadow or through the neighboring forest. Each space greets you in its own language. The day is at zenith. Grasses surround you, long like hair. You walk and recall a song. Ants run over your route. Grasshoppers dart, flying sideways from under your feet.

Flowers astound us with their smell. They retreat, bending backward out of your way. The heat is like that of a bath. Space itself swims toward you to spread under your feet. You walk thus for a long time across the meadow or the sparse forest. Ants run over your route.

Suddenly you are gripped by the premonition of irremediable misfortune: time prepares to stop. The day falls upon you like lead. The catalepsy of time! The world stands before you like a member. You look around: how dead is the bloom everywhere! With horror and dread you wait for the explosion. And the explosion comes.

"The explosion comes?"

"Yes. You hear your name called. (Gogol talks about that.)"

They all had a drink. And the diminutive Greek asked: "Why?" They smiled.

"Because you entered Dead Water. Dead Water is dense water that closes over your head like a rock. You walked easy as song. You entered an overcrowded day, where light, smell, and heat are at a limit. They stand like thick rays, like horns. There is no division there, no motion, no sequence. This water is hard as a rock.

"But who called you by name? You yourself, of course. In mortal fear you remembered the final factor, with both hands you grabbed onto your soul. Be proud, you were present at reverse rotation."

"Is this not," said the fourth speaker, "what all tales of the sleeping kingdom intend to tell? Do you remember the kingdom in which even the clock stops and the valet stands still with saucer in hand? Also the attic with a dormer window, the resentful old lady, and the drop of blood from the pinprick? For the time being the whole kingdom overgrows with trees and flowers. But what does the pinprick have to do with it? Truth to tell, I don't take it upon myself to explain the tale, it's too timorous and inarticulate.

"Yet in the end the explanation has to do with curve of resistance that is not in the drawing. The curve that regulates all our sensations, magnifying and diminishing them. In other words, it creates time. If it's not time that gives birth to articulate thought, what does?

"I want to say that if all states had the same intensity, then life would have flowed into one infinite world, like a swallow, like the sound of a tuning fork. Plants differ from animals in that for plants time doesn't exist.

"Isn't this why you need a pinprick? It lets the blood out. Slowly leaving its prison, the blood starts its unindividuated life, the life of flowers and trees."

"I know of another life that also wanted to pour out and dissolve time," said the champion. "I am speaking of Buddha. Poor Buddha, he too was born in the south and he too stopped before the north border. Why does he sit with his legs crossed, as if inside a uterus? He wants to become a watery sphere."

"Yes, there is a special form which is the same as horror," said the captain. "It approaches the parabola."

"It exists in the zeppelin, the basin, and the bedbug."

"Let us discuss this circumstance," said the fourth speaker.

INVESTIGATION OF HORROR

"I once saw a young girl who ran out from the table at time of dinner. Her mouth gaped sideways and, her fingers spread wide apart, she froze in meaningless horror.

"On a spacious white dish in the maid's beautiful hands lay the slightly trembling jelly. It resembled a deep-sea monster, just hauled up by fishermen's nets from some lightless and frigid abyss. It still retained the unstable form of a jellyfish. Its shudder was like shallow and frequent breathing; slow death.

"It was suffocating."

"In the roster of animals evoking horror, almost all have no legs or many.

"The spider: spherical belly hanging off eight thin, oscillating, whiskerlike legs. The octopus: muscular and malevolent spider of the sea. The crab: spider that sprouted an exoskeleton. Cockroach, centipede, plated millipede, bedbug, louse—all these black, red, transparent droplets moving their whiskers of legs one after another. The only exception is the bat, a black homunculus entangled in its own wings."

"The tank: why does the sight of a tank put to flight whole regiments of men? Because of its caterpillar treads. You can get an idea of this by turning over a bottle of castor oil or olive oil: the contents pour in slow, continuous stream. What if it also were churning? So move the screws of machines: they protrude, then they draw back into their metallic beds. They flow. If there were liquid animals, this is what their motion would have been like.

"The toad's stomach recalls jelly. The human behind also. That poor girl who got so scared of dessert, how much more would have been frightened had she, entering the room at the wrong hour, caught the maid with her brother? For then human bodies resemble two deep-sea monsters meeting each other again after long separation. And their movements are as the movements of a caterpillar in the final molt before chrysalis.

"The young girl notices how the white headpiece on the maid's head rocks to and fro."

"All these creatures are related to darkness. Darkness fashioned their body, it enters its form and consistency. You can see that right away. But doesn't it also determine their gait? Their gait at once obnoxious and uncertain, the torso motionless: that gait with clear and sudden stops and changes of direction—always going side-ways, aslant. This is how you move feelingly. Thus runs, for exam-ple, a rat—as if wound up. It runs as if it were slipping down an incline."

"You were saying there is no such thing as liquid animals," said the fourth speaker. "There almost are. I mean our intestines. What makes intestines so disgusting? Their movement. Yet all the things we have been talking about terrify precisely by their particular mode of movement.

"Their mode of movement is called peristalsis. Add vertigo (when everything swims before us and within us), the fear felt at falling, and the fear of dead men. We are terrified of formless life, the life of emptiness. Alas, I say nothing new. Why?"

Here ends the investigation of horror.

Still, you can reason otherwise. You believe that in the open steppe there is a large village; on its edge, in the way of the wind, stands a quadrangular hut. In that hut lives Horror. He sits and spins on a spindle, he sings and works through the night. The tales he sings of inspire wonder. But why was a young man placed there to do the job of a woman? Beasts, plants, and lines approach the dark porch. They try to look into the window. They ask each other: "Who is it there, singing so beautifully? Who is the warbler that doesn't skimp on his strength?"

So you can reason like this as well.

The diminutive Greek started blinking: "I want to tell my tale."

THE DIMINUTIVE GREEK'S TALE

"This is the story of my calamities. When my wife used to fall asleep—now she is dead—I would quietly put on slippers and go out into the bathroom. My wife slept in her bed fully dressed. Why did I see her from the other room? I swear to you, I saw her from the other room through a closed door. She was sleeping in low light, my small one, my creature of God. Who can tell me what this means: she was sleeping. A human being is close but also further away than if in a different solar system. And if you love this human being . . ."

"If you were liquids, you would have known what to do. You would have become a solution."

"Yes, if we were liquids. But damn you, captain, together with your advice. Not knowing what to do, I embraced the bath's cold water heater.

"Then I returned to the room and threw back the covers before switching off the light . . . The body lay before me, what am I saying, the soul itself lay before me. Wave, soul, petal, sunspot, the soul itself lay on the bedsheet in front of me, blossoming with hair, with rays of arms and legs, with mounds of breasts, with stalks and reeds of blood vessels. So the soul lay before me like an oyster. . . .

"The ship was stuffy. She went uneven and heavy. I swayed in a hammock next to sick, vomiting passengers. At each blow our hammocks swung apart and then sped toward each other like the two pendulums of adjacent clocks. It was half dark. Old men and women spread their sandwiches out on dirty benches. Wide plashes of waves advanced on the ship. The ship rocked like a rotten egg. But I was not angry: I knew that such was the thought of the sea. It bore us to a strange country.

"We went into port just before noon. Heat reigned over the city. Bronzed scoundrels sat at café tables on the embankment, legs crossed. They spoke their lingua franca and ashed right into the water. You might have expected anything from them. Am I wrong? They had rubbed out their memory of themselves. They were slapping their knees and ostentatiously throwing money upon the table. They themselves were like money: exchanging hands and unaware of mercy. Thick glasses full of multicolored wine stood before them like pharmaceutical alembics.

"Not far from a building I noticed a palm. A naked black man with graying temples sat under it, typing. A parrot cage hung right there, tied by a rope to the palm trunk. The parrot in the cage had its head cocked in wordless melancholy."

(The diminutive Greek went on talking in the same vein.)

At this time a young man rose from the nearby table and approached the speakers, greeting them with a bow:

"I come to you as the ambassador of a friendly nation. I am certain that you labor over most vital and noble questions, without even suspecting that you are laboring. My friends entrusted me to suggest: Why don't we join our tables? It doesn't matter which of us will reach the finish line first. We will become one, like two liquids."

"We are very grateful for the invitation," said the fourth speaker. "We are discussing the antitheses of south and north. It is an endless topic indeed. The questions we pose to Nature are head-on, and she has no right to ignore them. She responds with exact answers, exact albeit incomprehensible. But look, it is already late. The orchestra is playing the final works on its song list. Why should we magnify the work of waiters?"

"Of course, you are right," said the young man. "As far as we are concerned, we study plumages. We try to decode that voice with which Nature speaks freely and clearly. She speaks by grass and by leaves: yes, I exist as one wave. She speaks or sings by the color yellow: I am a cross section, I am a record. We are currently amazed at the possible meanings of the blue underwings of a spotted moth from the family *Noctuidae*.

"We are putting together something of a small dictionary, studying faces and facial expressions of all things. And so, good luck to you."

"You think I remember nothing," continued the diminutive Greek. "No, I remember everything. At my wife's funeral it was very windy. I walked the whole road without a hat, like an idiot."

FOURTH SPEAKER: Be not upset by these terrible memories. The grief that you were not able to process on time now poisons every one of your days. But I give you my word: an extraordinary joy awaits all of us, joy we cannot even expect.

"Happiness is a beet sugar factory," said one of them. "The plantations extend all the way to the sky and even enter it."

"Happiness is flying from trapeze to trapeze," said another. "When you feel no weight, velocity ceases to exist and you swim through glistening space like a starfish."

"Happiness is a sailboat," said the third. "She does not feel movement. You think you are sailing over sea. I wonder whether you are not sailing along time. The sunset's yellow strip spreads so close by as to seem within effortless reach."

"None of this lies beyond reach," said the champion. "When the diminutive Greek has made his money, he will buy beet sugar factories with plantations to the very horizon and also a sailboat; he'll set up trapezes under the big top of his room. Then he'll know these things with greater precision. We are indeed putting together a small dictionary and I think we are approaching the junction. Anyhow, happiness belongs to friable and unsteady environments. It is said that when ants celebrate a major holiday, they climb up a steep sand-hill and then slide down. And why does the dog, when it feels joy, turn over, waving its four paws in the air? I think this is not a bad business concept: to set up haylofts at holiday resorts. At any rate, what is the difference between the restaurant and the canteen? Restaurants give you vertigo."

"How beautiful everything is in this restaurant. Waiters, as serious as angels, appear here and there among the tables. Women with faces of flowers bend over the bell-mouthed glasses. And there: behold the sonic sun in the semicircle. It pulsates just like the real sun. There are many different sources of illumination here, like at a bay at night. There are more smells than in a tropical forest here. The patrons are eating unhurried—like victors, like scholars. There are liquids here, rubber and glass. There are reflections, rapids, rotations; there is diversity of space.

"The fish doesn't know it's moving when it works its fins. It thinks it's shoveling ocean. Or, it thinks: 'My fins alter the face of the ocean.' Musicians believe they control the music. They are wrong. Time moves through their instruments, through strings and through hollow tubes, through bronchi and fingers. Look at how they rock, how they dance. Time moves in pity and joy through forms of resistance. Occasionally you hear whistles and horns, for the railroad is nearby. Yet when we die, we'll find ourselves at a train station. It will not be entirely unlike a regular train station. And what awaits us afterward? An unbelievable flowering? Or the same old thing? Will we turn into number, underwater birds, sea currents? What awaits us afterward, I ask you. Oven or garden? Or will we promenade over a sand-strewn path and draw all the stories of the world upon it without paying attention to wind?"

"I've always loved poems," said the captain and covered the speakers in smoke. "Once, when I was a kid, they took me somewhere in a cab. The carriage rode alongside a tram and could neither overtake it nor fall behind. I was seized with some kind of joy. It seemed that the whole city with all its churches and bridges fit in my round palm. I think this resembles that famous sensation of déjà vu—false memory."

"It resembles everything," said the champion. "It resembles memory, it resembles the tropical sensation, it resembles rubber gloves and many other things."

"I myself loved poems," continued the champion. "Once, when I was a kid, I was riding a tram through a foreign city. Summer rain was falling at a slant, and I noticed that the moist tramcar windows made the city look especially beautiful. Then I arrived at the train station. At the station there was the usual bustle; trains were pulling in and recoiling from posts dug into the ground; people were running in different directions, their trajectories crossing. 'Could it be,' I thought, 'that in several minutes I'll be suddenly gone from this station? No, that's impossible.'

"So many years have passed since then, yet need I tell you that I never again set foot in that foreign city? And it remained as it was under that slanted rain—still bright through wet tramcar windows. Yet still I think that even now I am standing at the train station, anticipating the passing future.

"A mad hope for encounter will not let me alone. For the wave moves up and down and yet does not leave its place."

"Water is the same as light," said the champion. "Note that in legends dead men were ferried over dark water. They forget everything. Of course, now we would have said: time; but back then we said: water. I don't know which is more right. What if the subterranean waters are luminous?"

"For the shores he is Charon," said the captain, "but in Russian we might have called him: old crone. The old crone patiently steers the ferry with his pole. He stinks of onions. Little villagers stand off to the sides in throngs, nodding off into sleep. They don't give a damn that they are traversing Lethe. They don't remember anything anyway."

"In the olden days they put dead men into boats," said the diminutive Greek, "and pushed the boats off to the sea. Leave-takers crowded on the shore, giving all sorts of advice and acting possessed by demons. It is said that winds and currents took some boats as far as America. Then they started putting hay into boats and setting it afire. Fire sailed over the water and men found it easier to turn into smoke."

FOURTH SPEAKER: If we wanted to draw a dream, it would look like a watery sphere. Because the dream is the only example we have in our lives of a closed system, not counting games. The strangest thing for me is that the dreamer lies like a log, and at the same time he is a hero turning all sorts of tricks. And you can see him from every side. He sees himself from the side. His is the initial projection, prior even to space.

In this exact sense must we understand the expression: the big dream dreams of being the little dream, the little dream that dreams of being the big dream. Yet the little dream dreams the big dream in parts. Here's a diagram: [cylinder].

CHAMPION: Our conversation is at an end. Our closed system is at an end. Let us run the analysis.

In the middle of the sea a cargo ship waits. The only two passengers are at cards in its hot hold. The loser looks at the guy who cleaned him out with utter despair. But he shows no mercy. That look is the diminutive Greek.

Now for the captain. Three times he crossed the sea forward and backward. Well does he know his thrice-repeated contemptible murder. But on your tanned face there is not even a shadow of repentance. That's fine. The cocks have not crowed as yet: they feel an acrid disgust. What about me, the champion? I am the conversation that decided it exists.

DIMINUTIVE GREEK [*after a slight pause*]: So what is the outcome of our conversation?

FOURTH SPEAKER: You know the parable of the man who got a check for a large sum. He used to buy goods in just one store, say, a shoe store, and so he thought his check was for shoes. Then he discovered that the check was for money: that is to say for nothing, for anything. He was glad.

Or else: even in our lifetimes we can get a pretty precise idea of how the world looks to our friends who have already died. This, perhaps, is the only outcome of our conversation.

DIMINUTIVE GREEK: But what does it mean for us?

FOURTH SPEAKER: It doesn't bode well, believe me.

Early 1930s
Translated by Eugene Ostashevsky

Yakov Druskin

Death

When before death he kept saying, "it hurts," it came out as "he hurts." When his face grimaced with pain, it was something like a reflex, and you knew his soul was not in pain. The day before death he answered all questions with "good," and he also said, "the hands are good, the feet are good, and in the earth it's good."

He pulled the sheet over his face and when asked why, said, "to set the mood." When the sheet was taken away, he covered his face with his hands.

He died four times over two weeks. The first death looked entirely wise from the side, that was when he said, "the shoulder is tired, the arm is tired, everything is tired." The second death took place in total silence, he was growing colder and weaker. The third death occurred over twenty-four hours, he kept repeating, "it's all good," and he said, "now I am going to sleep." After this he fell asleep and then lay unconscious with eyes open. The fourth death was the most terrifying and incomprehensible. I think he was fully conscious.

When he lay dying the fourth time, perhaps two hours before the last death a certain understanding came: not a word was said, he could not speak, but he passed on to me his legacy and seniority in the family. I saw that he knew it as well as I. It was as a kind of justification and transfer of legacy and seniority in the family, as a kind of harbinger of the final hour and the laying on of the seal. I never understood anything as clearly in my life.

He died four times, he sought the most favorable means of death and chose the most incomprehensible and terrifying: a gurgling of the chest and an outpouring of froth. Perhaps there lay the least peccadillo.

When death came to him the first time, he stared straight ahead of himself, noticing nothing and saying nothing. What did he see? Maybe he was directing all his strength to the healing of his heart? The fourth time he also stared without noticing anything, but it was different, there was horror in it, or maybe it was I who was terrified. But then he looked at me, it was when he passed on to me the seniority in the family. His gaze was clear and conscious. It came from one eye, the other was paralyzed.

Whenever his condition improved a little, he started to worry, begging us to call him a doctor. But when it got very bad, when he felt death approaching, he acted calm, indifferent to doctors' visits, and said he was good even though he knew he was dying.

Maybe what I called the second death came first, and the first second?

August third he fell ill. At night I ran with Lida to the nurse's across the field. Under heavy rain to Kozmin's; at the hospital searching for the doctor.

The fourth. Strong pain until six. After six the pain went away, the night calm except he tossed violently and constantly.

The fifth. Seemed to deteriorate again, in the evening grows cold, without pulse, hot bottles at night. The first death, I think.

The sixth. Second death. Improved in the evening, but at night, nightmares.

The ninth. Possibly getting better.

The tenth to the thirteenth. Gradual deterioration.

The fourteenth. I went to the city for the day. As I was leaving he complained of the slowness of his recovery. When I came back in the evening, he was in a very bad way. I spent the night running after oxygen (don't remember when I did it the first time). The first attack. In the morning seemed asleep with eyes open.

The fifteenth. All day with his eyes open, either asleep or unconscious. Recognizes only by hearing. Speaks very little, with difficulty and indistinctly. Second attack at 3:00 or 4:00 A.M. Then—fully aware, but his speech as inarticulate as before, was saying good-bye to us. Then said he was going to sleep and fell into sleep or coma with his eyes open. Stayed like that until morning: I think his left side became paralyzed then.

The sixteenth. Pulse reappeared, quite good, he came to, asked who was with him. Then he spoke no more, it was too hard to speak, but he pointed. I think it was then that he asked to have the curtain raised and the window opened. Or maybe he had asked earlier, I don't remember. His eyes gradually became glassy, especially the one that was paralyzed. Late in the day or in the evening the third attack came, not one but several. In the evening he could no longer move. At eleven or midnight the gurgling in the chest began—pulmonary edema, I am almost certain that from then on he was fully conscious. Around four he looked at me. At half past five came the last attack. During the attack his breathing became stop-and-go, he was out of air, his gaze was conscious and you could see the horror. After the last attack his heart stopped but there were two or three more breaths, and his eyes became calm again.

I stand before an event of the fullest reality, this is why I am afraid to say anything, everything is dubious and worthless before it.

In the evening of the second day of his illness he felt better. I left for a little while. Returning by horse-drawn cab I saw an elderly man with a cane. He was walking with his wife. The sight was like a sign of times past, of a certain respectability which is no longer there. That's what happiness is—to run into your parents, elderly people occupying a modest place; it was happiness when, for instance, they saw me off or they met me in Pushkin as I came from the city to be with them for several hours. When I saw the couple I understood: happiness is no more.

And yet that certain feeling of well-being and tranquillity had disappeared even earlier. The horror of its death united with the horror before the modern-day Leviathan.

As any direction, once taken, points straight ahead, whereas reverse motion lies in the realm of possibility only, so, perhaps, happiness and the happy life are always what was and will not be.

Up to 1917 life seemed to improve every year. Those who called it progress neglected something profound and important. After several difficult postwar years life became light and empty like that of mayflies, but there was also the sensation of talent and genius. And then all this collapsed at once. Now that sensation of tranquillity and improvement neither is nor can be. The old and the new differ in essence and the difference is like that of his death.

At certain instances you can't say: God exists but gods and demons do not. At certain instances you can't say: gods and demons exist. At certain instances you can't say: there are omens and following them creates favorable circumstances. At certain instances you can't say: there are no omens. I sacrificed to a god. After some time I understood: the god accepted my sacrifice and the circumstances were favorable. This god was the god of health, hearth, and the happy life, the god of meeting between parents and their adult son.

I am no longer careful. I frequently disobey omens, transgress against rules of precaution. The indicators got tangled up.

If I say: a god has accepted my sacrifice, I was in contact with gods and demons—these are signs. The same with God, with immortality—they too are signs. You must choose the signs with the least peccadillo.

Is death accidental? Would he have died now, under different circumstances?

One time when I had some problem, I thought: this is what they mean by calamity. It went on for several days. But then I left for Pushkin. When I woke up in the morning I saw the trees and the sun in the window and I thought: I feel good. No problem, no calamity. August seventeenth after his death the day was bright and sunny, but to me the sunlight seemed to have lost its strength. And I am afraid the sun will never shine as before.

I think about him all the time, when I walk, read, go somewhere, and all the time I see those two final hours and that moment when he passed on to me his legacy and the seniority in the family. But today on my way home I thought: it just can't be that I'll never see him again, I'll see him in three years or thirty; I am so stupid for not having remembered it earlier. This thought came from firm conviction in personal immortality. Should the conviction disguise the beginning of oblivion, should it be only a feint of feeling and attraction to life, then life is meaningless and disgusting.

Death must find its place in a certain system. I myself am that system, and the death is not any death but a definite one. Oblivion does not consist of forgetting the man but of forgetting the grief. First of all, I need to get used to the fact that many accidental things, many accidental events have changed. When I approach the clock to wind it, I remember how he wound it; when I approach the window, I remember how he stood by the window. I need to remember and maybe to perform every thing he did. But there's something else: I will never see him again and this "never" is terrifying. Immortality must exist.

Tiutchev has it that death and sleep are twins, and suicide and love also twins. Habit and oblivion, these too are twins.

If oblivion does not come from conviction in personal immortality and the meeting to come, then this feint of attraction to life is abominable.

When I used to hear that a man died, even a stranger, for several seconds I would sink into melancholy and anguish. Abomination of desolation, that's what death is. Now this feeling won't go away and I will always remember how in the final minute he clenched his teeth and there was horror in his eyes. Then the heart stopped, and he breathed several times freely and tranquilly. The abomination of desolation after his death, it is like tentacles from the other world.

The unique, unrepeatable thing is that the flower used to be beautiful. But it wilted and rotted. The abomination of desolation does not diminish from the survival of other, even more beautiful flowers: this one is gone. Can you say that the whole is beautiful? What whole? This flower, this field, right now. But the whole is incomprehensible within time. Time bears death.

I discover the beautiful as it is arranged in space but not in time. And music? When one sound follows another, I discover here a certain system of the particular, I do not apprehend one sound as coming after another, but in the last sound, the sound I just heard, I discover the previous ones. This is not the same as joining the moments borne by time. The duration of a piece of music may be classified as a slight peccadillo, for the piece is already written and exists as a whole, I can apprehend it entirely, I can even learn it by heart. I see it as God sees it. But the life of a flower, that I do not see, and I do not apprehend myself in time, but only in the moment. Yet if God sees my whole life, he sees it at once, that is to say not in time. God does not see time, whereas I experience time as a certain defect. The comparison with a piece of music goes only so far, because the piece apprehends itself neither as a whole nor in each note, whereas I do apprehend myself, but only in the moment.

Beautiful is the flight of a seagull. Its motion occurs also in time but perhaps it is beautiful because we apprehend it as an immobile line in space? And in such things as riding fast or swimming, time and change are felt perhaps least of all. The surf rolling in or out, the sound of the sea or the forest, the periodicity of nature—all these invoke a certain horror. Maybe time is not even continuous. When we talk about the continuous nature of time, we immediately refer to the line in order to explain temporal continuity. Therefore the continuous nature of time is not by any means self-evident.

One can say what is not in time, but how can one say what time is? Not any of the words that apply to things that exist can be applied to time; we may even say that it does not exist. But this nonexistent thing is the most frightening of powers and you feel best when you don't feel it.

Nor do I understand when they say that something exists in time. Something exists in the moment, whereas in time it is destroyed and ceases to exist.

They also speak of duration. This creature of time is entirely devoid of reality. It exists only in order to be halted by the moment.

From the fact that I can find beauty in spatial arrangement whereas time bears only death and decay, although it itself cannot be grasped and does not even exist and does not permit anything else to exist in it, follows the incommensurability of space and time.

The moment is the only reality. Then there are also memory, imagination, and reason. All of them can be united under the name of ideas. They are the signs of moments. They put a stop to duration, they divide it. When I find the right sign, I name the moment, and motion and duration halt, they cease to exist, they become what they are, that is: nothing. For they do not exist in the moment, and nothing exists apart from the moment.

In the beginning God created heaven and earth. The beginning is a certain halt, cut, sign, it is the archetype of the moment.

Although the noise of the sea or the forest invokes a certain horror by its periodicity, we don't apprehend it as a temporal phenomenon either. Constant repetition of the same thing creates the sensation of immobility. At first it appears to increase distances but then it creates definite borders.

A happy life differs from an unhappy one not in its main events but in its secondary ones—by a hardly noticeable tint.

I started to experience a certain freedom: I do not always take precautionary measures, and if I do take them, then my heart is not in it. The freedom that could have offered a certain tranquillity results instead in a repellent emptiness. I was entangled in the nets of omens and indicators. There was fear, but there was also tranquillity and joy. I felt a certain link with what exists. But now the nets are torn.

In Leonid Andreev, Lazarus lay in the crypt for several days before his resurrection and he swelled up. He rose swollen and stayed swollen, and whoever he looked at felt empty and bored. His gaze made men wither.

Dreams.

1. He starts to recover, he is walking, for full recovery they send him to Finland.—Yet how can he travel alone, he is ill. I go to the station to buy a ticket for me as well and suddenly halt.—It's too late, he can't be saved anyway, he'll die just as he died the first time. I experience inevitability.

2. The four of us are in a room. I leave, go to the morgue and look for him there. Instead I find two corpses—both of boys: one lies contorted, his stomach on a trunk, his feet touching the floor. Suddenly I remember: but he was still alive when Mama left two

days ago, she told me to look after him and I forgot. Maybe he died alone—then I remember how he lay like a larva or a striped caterpillar. I flee. I feel the boy cadaver behind me, in pursuit. He runs contorted, just as he lay.

3. He starts to recover, he even gets up. I think: now we won't permit what happened before, that is, his death. Still, some thought is bothering me, but not the thought of his death, since I know he already died once, even though now he is alive. Gradually the thought clarifies and I remember that we buried him, that we piled earth over him, and therefore he can never be alive again, even if I do see him with my own eyes.

When I dream of something, then, in order to ascertain that it's not just a dream and delirium, that my sense of reality isn't playing tricks on me, I start to recall the past and to relate events. In dreams the remembered event is reexperienced, that is to say, time does not exist there, whereas in reality such an event is completed, no longer existent, destroyed by time. In dreams it is waking that appears most real—when I dream I am waking, I recall the prior dream as an event that has ended.

I drew a line around myself, I had words that I repeated constantly, and I knew that I could be tranquil so long as I observed omens and remained within this circle. The circle diminishes distances, creates a certain order and well-being in life. During his illness, the only important thing was that he does not die. But now the circle is broken.

Some dreams are so simple and distinct that when you wake up you wonder whether it's worth making the effort to remember them, and in the morning you forget them. Meanwhile, these dreams are often interesting, some for their content, others by tone. Thoughts, like dreams, also have content and tone. Certain thoughts are interesting for their tone, and these are the hardest to write down.

Lack of joy in existence blasphemes against the Holy Spirit, for God, after he created the heaven and the earth, said they were good. Blasphemy against the Holy Spirit will not be forgiven.

A dream. After that incident (that is to say, his illness and death) he began to recover. I asked, "Can it be that a man died and was buried, and then began to recover and came back?" He answered nothing, but he started to disappear before my eyes. I went through incredible efforts to make him stay, I didn't look aside, I didn't blink, but it was all in vain.

Every day I wait for a miracle, and especially before sleep and during the night I ask God for a miracle. Miracles must exist.

It is already two and a half months that God abandoned me. God abandoned me twenty-four hours before his death.

I was sitting at night by the open window and crying, thinking of how I accomplished nothing of what he wanted: I have not stopped smoking, I have not gotten my degree, I have not created a place for myself in life, and at that moment I felt God abandon me. It really was like a slight breath of the air.

The day of death is accidental, it could have come earlier or later. How to understand this? I will introduce a term. It does not explain a lot, but perhaps it will show the way to a certain understanding. Extending momentary existence along immobile time, certain events can be called the characters of a life. Death coming too early can be one of them, death coming too late, another.

Maybe there exist different kinds of time. There is the time of thinking and the time of living, the time of the participant in life and the time of the man standing off to the side. There is the time of self-awareness—it is no longer than a moment—and the time of recollection, when two times coincide.

Time does not last and does not go on, it is made up of moments and empty intervals.

I take a segment of time. During this time, I was traveling—I walked a certain distance. At the time of walking I noticed a certain uniformity of one particular part of my journey and ascribed another part of my journey to another segment of time. I differentiated one segment of time from another. This happens when you make the same journey over and over again, when you walk the same road many times a day, many days. This segment of time I will call the large moment. Time is missing from it.

If there exists a certain harmonious order and well-being, and this is equivalent to the fact that God exists, then its criterion can only be my own well-being—a certain harmonious order of whatever pertains to me.

I imagine three systems of things. The first is founded on trust. But if I doubt and lack trust, what am I to do? The second is founded on reason. But if I am feeble and my abilities are limited, I can commit an ineradicable error. I am guilty according to the first, I am guilty according to the second.

According to the third system everyone is guilty.

A dead man on the shore of the river of oblivion says: I died just now, I died yesterday, I died a thousand years ago. When my heart stopped I breathed once or twice. I breathed the last time. Between two breaths my soul separated itself from my body. The soul of a dead man on the shore of the river of oblivion says: I am being lied to, I am being buried. A moment passes, a year passes, a thousand years pass. I observe time flattened, the events strewn over it at random. The past weighs on me, it stands before me like an immobile now, like a large moment, it is cold here and deserted. The dead man on the shore of the river of oblivion weeps over his body:

how my arm was beautiful, warm, white. How my belly was beautiful, convex, soft. My chest and my neck were beautiful. He is sorry he can't raise his head, move his arm.

No freshness of feelings.

If a system exists—a certain order and correspondence—in which I cannot observe myself as an end, then such a system is amoral. That is, I should not be a means. If there exists eternal condemnation—expulsion from a certain system—it is hard to understand, for instance, if I have not trust.

Lipavsky invented a formula for incomprehension: the father does not understand the son. But as far as the horror of death is concerned, that is to say, the cooling of the arm, the numbness, the withering, here the son does not understand the father.

As perhaps the soul survives the body for a certain time, so the soul of pleasure can be separated from pleasure. But it can also be that for a long time, perhaps forever, the soul of pleasure lies dead or asleep. Then the pleasure amounts to nothing.

I want to know about the dead man in the grave, how he lies there, and where his soul is.

There exist errors of right reasoning and right inference.

If a single step already taken in life were reversible, then, all other circumstances equal, it would seem no greater miracle than the opening of a bud, the growth of a tree, or the might of political power. Meanwhile there would be more seriousness in it, and responsibility.

The contrary of a miracle is not natural necessity but compulsion. Miracles can be neither imagined nor investigated. A miracle under investigation loses everything miraculous about it. It is what no investigation can trap.

Two errors: the error of ambivalence arises from forgetting a certain outside force that opposes your desires. Another error, close to the error of right reasoning, arises from framing that force as the law of nature, as natural necessity.

Heraclitus says: There is something that old age buys for the price of life. He must mean wisdom.

To start afresh over and over, as if I did not understand anything yesterday or as if yesterday did not take place.

A dream. He was running quickly up the stairs, jumping over two or three at once. I got scared: "What are you doing, you can't go up the stairs so fast, you'll get sick and die again." He suddenly changed, shrank, and I again experienced inevitability.

The final night of August seventeenth there was a concert in the community center across the street. We could hear the music.

For me that which exists has decomposed into its final elements, and these elements are: the cooling of the arm, the immobility of the body, silence, death.

I looked for that which is always new. Death is that which is always new.

What do I care whether I am foolish or wise, if there is no happiness.

One time I wrote, "Even upon universal ruins and remnants . . ." So I aimed to prove the existence of God. But now universal ruins and remnants are upon me and I see nothing.

Truth degree zero. This must be the ultimate, final truth, when there are no more desires, aims, tastes, inclinations. But then there is probably nothing at all.

At the bedside of the dying man I saw that life itself is the supreme good, and that the cooling of the arm, withering, and death are abominations. But now I do not feel the good, I do not feel that my life is a good.

When the soul of pleasure died and life ceased to interest me, I saw that life is a good in itself, the supreme good.

Pleasures may be classified; pleasure from food, sleep, etc., may even be defined, but happiness is unique and therefore escapes definition and classification. It comes at random and differs for everybody. When I said that the happy life is the life of coastal dwellers, this was not a definition of happiness but one of its names. Happiness may be unhappy, pleasure invokes interest. If there is happiness, there is love of life, but there is no love of life in pleasure without happiness.

Wisdom lies in thinking of happy life once it is lost forever, and in the art of living without happiness.

A firm foundation exists in that which stands. Interpret it so: the life of messengers is no more illusory than natural necessity. Absence is no more illusory than presence. And also: a certain motion, a certain fulfilled desire, a certain thought carried to its end—these are illusory. And all of these are one—a certain moment when that moment expires.

The sign of a dream consists in the absence of the firm and the solid. To the firm and the solid belong: my bed, my room, familiar voices, sounds, and objects. After the best of sleeps you wake up content, experiencing restoration to the firm and the solid, provided that all firmness and solidity have not been lost, and these are the minimum amount of happiness necessary for a life.

Lipavsky asked: "Can you feel that half your life has passed?" I said: "I feel that my whole life has passed." Lipavsky: "Isn't it time for us to think about the soul?" I: "Maybe there's nothing to think about." Lipavsky: "Now that immortality appears unnecessary, perhaps we will find that it really exists."

One cannot pray to a passionless God.

Chance does not create any order, it is the seal of indifference upon time. Who places it? I don't know. It was foreseen by God, but it does not get placed altogether without my participation. But I cannot foresee what lies far ahead and sometimes I act inattentively. If anything exists that is indeed firm and solid, events do not change it, it lies outside events.

A slight peccadillo grew into a big lie.

Four rules:
1. Make the least amount of effort.
2. Maintain the monotony of my life.
3. Observe seriousness, that is, avoid events, decisions, actions and interactions with people as much as possible.
4. Avoid pleasures requiring effort.

A dream. I dreamed that I was at the cemetery, I approached the grave, I raised my head and I saw, in fear, that there was no monument. It vanished.

Several days later I really did go to the cemetery. Approaching the grave I remembered my dream and again felt the same fear. I raised my head and saw that the monument wasn't there. It vanished.

A dream. Georg again came in the night and taught me to walk backward and forward in time and this was as simple as going from one room to another.

I understood something from that dream. It was him but as if under another name. The dream proved rigorously and incontrovertibly that he did not die. And yet he died. An indefinite sign of an incontrovertible, evident proof turned out fruitless and useless.

Truth degree zero lies outside the system, but outside the system nothing is firm and solid. Condemnation means expulsion from the system. But any other truth requires some trust.

When you experience some sufficiently strong feeling or sensation several times, then at the moment of each experience you cannot say how often you felt it before, and therefore the location of events along the axis of time lacks fixity.

One needs to distinguish between pleasure, happiness, and the soul of pleasure. If the sensation of pleasure survives the pleasure for a certain time, then this sensation is the soul of pleasure. Something must then exist between pleasure and its soul, and it is happiness, at least the minimum amount of happiness necessary for life.

Here are certain large moments. Many times a day I not walked but ran to the pharmacy for oxygen. The road went in a straight line to a big building. This interval for me became a large moment. Then one had to make several turns. There was a bar across the street from the pharmacy, music played there and drunken voices could be heard late into the night. At night to run past this bar was a large moment. The stairs I ascended not knowing whether I would find him alive was a large moment. In the night at the window when God abandoned me was a large moment. During one of the first days, when he felt better, I went for a walk. This last walk when the sun still shone with its former intensity was a large moment. After this for maybe two weeks I did not notice the sun shining. Whereas on August seventeenth I saw sunlight again, but it did not seem bright, it lost its intensity for the first time, and this too was a large moment.

August 17, 1935
A year passed. I lost the minimum amount of happiness necessary for life. Even if I gain it back, if some rational order is present in all this, what can compensate for the lost year of my life? Besides, I don't expect that next year will be any better.

August 1934—August 1935
Translated by Eugene Ostashevsky

Letter to Kharms

Dear Daniil Ivanovich, the messengers have abandoned me. I cannot even tell you how it happened. I was sitting at night by the open window and the messengers were still with me, and then they weren't. It is already three years that they are gone. I occasionally feel the approach of messengers but something prevents me from seeing them, or maybe it is they who are afraid. I think I have to make some effort, perhaps some minor effort, and at the same time to lie, and then the messengers will be with me again. But it is disgusting to lie to oneself and to messengers.

I used to think: maybe inspiration plays tricks on me. For I am a philosopher, I must write when I am calm and have no desires. I had wanted to write a dictionary or a compendium of investigations, and each would have started thus: "Here is what the disciple of Thales said when the master fell silent, for inspiration abandoned him." Now, when there are no desires, no inspiration, and the messengers have abandoned me, I see there is nothing to write or think about. But maybe I am wrong, maybe it's just the kind of day I'm having: I feel the proximity of messengers but am unable to see them.

Summer 1937
Translated by Eugene Ostashevsky

» » » « « «

The End of the World

When a man dies slowly and, before that, he is ill for a long time, this is what's terrifying: every day he gets just a little worse, so that you even think he is getting better, but then you remember: a week ago he could get up by himself, yet now he can only turn over. Then you forget about it, but after some time you notice, with horror, that he can't even turn over, that he can only raise his head. That's when you first see the inevitability.

The same for the end of the world.

Maybe it will approach over the course of the year. It will certainly arrive in hot weather: begin in July and end in July. Maybe it will begin this way: one morning through the window or outside on the street I will see a man who seems indistinguishable from everyone else, except his gait will be a bit slower and more deliberate than that of the others. This is the kind of person you always notice and immediately forget. That's exactly what will happen this time as well. Others will also see him, and they too will notice him and immediately forget him: there'll be nothing miraculous about it, because he'll show up in different places at different times. The second time I see him I won't be surprised—maybe I won't even remember having seen him before. When I see him the third time a few days later, the thought will cross my mind that I have seen him before, but I'll soon forget him again. These encounters will recur over two weeks, from the first to the fifteenth of July. The final encounter will result in a vague anxiety, but then no one will see

237

him for the next two weeks. In the first days of August he'll be seen again. The first sighting will produce some surprise and even joy—the kind you feel when something familiar returns—but with more encounters the anxiety will grow, and it will have had turned to dread if the encounters won't have ceased on the fifteenth of August.

There are certain sensations that vanish when you become aware of them, but the moment that you stop thinking about them they reappear. So it will then be with the feeling of dread. No one will speak of the man, since to do so would seem foolish, just as it's foolish to talk about excessively vague premonitions and sensations. Yet I'll notice from the expressions on the faces of others, when in my presence they meet him in the street—maybe they'll be trying to walk past without brushing against him—or when talk turns to people afraid of space, it will suddenly occur to me that others are anxious about these encounters too. But no one will dare ask, because it's foolish to ask when there isn't any basis for questions: do you not have a premonition of something, something which is for that matter undefined. On the fifteenth of August the encounters will cease, and several days later everyone will have calmed down, although a certain tension, somewhat greater than usual, will remain. But at the beginning of September the encounters will resume, and this time—from the very first—they'll be accompanied by dread. Yet this dread will only be a premonition of the true dread to come. After several encounters, someone— maybe at some gathering of large groups of people or maybe in each individual home—will inadvertently say, remembering some event: "It happened around the time when the man who walks slowly first appeared." And this will be dread. The person who said it will suddenly stop, and everyone will understand that some horrifying and irrevocable thing has happened, and that everyone knows it. Yet they'll go on to talk of ordinary things, and any further discussion of the subject will now be considered in bad taste; but the feeling of dread will stay. Later they'll notice that more and more people are walking slowly, and it will seem that certain of their acquaintances are also walking more slowly. Perhaps they'll even notice that trains and trolleys are running more slowly and that the day is growing longer. The subject will be taboo, although the government, trying to calm everyone, will—as if incidentally—start to report the speed of trolleys, trains, and airplanes in newspapers; what's more, their speed will apparently have increased somewhat. Astronomical facts will be reported too, in order to prove that the length of the day has not changed. Simply, a cessation of movement will be in progress, but science won't be able to verify it because clocks will also be running more slowly. Then omens will start to appear but again with nothing of the miraculous in them, so that you can't even take them for omens: for example, the Neva sometimes falls a little below its yearly average water level and then rises back to the average, but that year it won't rise at all or will rise a few centimeters short. Or else, in the evening, heavy snow will fall, but it will completely melt by morning. Everyone's state will now be such that even the slightest chance occurrence, however natural, will instill fear. Spring will come very early, and the weather will be good. In March, April, and May, the sun will be bright; the showers brief; and there will be no gray, overcast days. But by then all will have noticed the slowing down of movement, that even birds fly more slowly; the contrast between a certain natural well-being and the human unease will fuel the dread: the sense of inevitability will become stronger. In fact, there will be something frightening about the promise of blue sky and hot, sunny days. The dread will grow so intense that people will no longer be able to distinguish between

the natural and unnatural. Then, one morning early in June, everyone will suddenly notice that the sun got larger. For the entire
month of June, the days will be hot and sunny, and, if rain comes,
it will only be so that people don't die before their time. Then in
July: doomsday.

1939
Translated by Thomas Epstein, Eugene Ostashevsky,
and Genya Turovskaya

Alexander Vvedensky

Only about fifty works by Vvedensky survive, but there is some information or remnant—often no more than a line—of at least as many others.
Confiscated during arrest, burned by friends afraid of police searches,
misplaced, or perhaps simply discarded by this poet who cared only about
the most recent of his work, their loss is a disaster for Russian literature,
for Vvedensky is, without a doubt, one of the most important Russian
poets of the twentieth century. This anthology includes mainly his final
pieces, those composed in Kharkov after his move there in 1936. A separate selection of his poems in our translation, entitled *An Invitation for Me
to Think,* is forthcoming in 2006 from Green Integer in Los Angeles.

Kuprianov and Natasha

This poem is dedicated to Vvedensky's breakup with Tatiana Meier
(1903–82), who later collaborated with Druskin on preserving and studying the legacy of the *chinars.*

6   *tuna*   In the original, pike perch.

11   *I never believed in any quantity of stars, / I believed in one star.*   A
corrected self-quotation of a poem addressed to Meier in 1920.

Rug/Hydrangea

The original is untitled, but "Rug/Hydrangea" is how the *chinars* referred
to it.

Frother

17   *Frother*   In the original, *potets*, a neologism composed of *pot* (sweat) and *otets* (father).

21   *pillow*   In Russian, *podushka,* accidentally like the Russian for "soul," *dusha.*

23   *The father sat atop a bronze steed . . .*   One of Vvedensky's many references to Pushkin's long poem *The Bronze Horseman,* the foundational text of the so-called Petersburg myth. For Vvedensky and Pushkin, whose work is sampled in just about every Vvedensky piece, see Gerasimova n.d.

A Certain Quantity of Conversations

28   *certain*   A common *chinar* term, indicating the imprecision inherent to any quantity. In Vvedensky's 1929 poem "Five or Six," a character proclaims: "That we actually have five or six horses I say purposefully approximately, since you can never say anything exact anyway."

38   *Debussy*   Puccini in the original, to rhyme with "about its deep" ("*o ego puchine*").

39   *Pushkin*   Allusion to Pushkin's fatal duel, which took place on January 27, 1837, near Chernaia Rechka (Black River) in St. Petersburg.

47   *Grand Duke K. R.*   Konstantin Romanov (1858–1915), Russian poet and grandson of Emperor Nicholas I.

Where. When.

The original is untitled.

Daniil Kharms

Daniil Yuvachov took the surname Kharms in high school in homage to Sherlock Holmes, transcribing it in the German manner as Charms to pun on the English words "harm" and "charm," the latter in all senses including "magic spell." His father once told him, "As long as your name is Kharms, you'll always get in harm's way!" Kharms's tastes were formed in part by English literature, especially Lewis Carroll and Edward Lear. He cultivated the appearance of an English eccentric, which in the paranoid 1930s took bravery and defiance. His diaries show him to have been quite religious.

The Measure of Things

Kharms assembled some of his texts in minicollections. The most famous of these is *Incidences,* translated in full by Neil Cornwell. "The Measure of Things," "The Saber," "The World," and "The Eleven Assertions of Daniil Ivanovich Kharms" (the latter in Kharms and Vvedensky 1997, 116–17) form about half of a cycle of mock-theoretical writings having to do with taking a personal, intuitive "measure" of the universe. They are thus about Kharms's view of poetry as well as other nonrational forms of knowing.

81   *slanting fathom*   In the original, *kosaia sazhen;* a Russian building
      measure equal to 83 inches or 213 cm.

The Saber

Kharms's references to numbers in developing his concept of measure derive from the concept of number as "plurality measurable by the one" in Greek philosophy (Aristotle *Metaphysics* 1057a4). Since the Greeks conceived of natural numbers as many ones, they had to answer the question of how we can recognize, say, three units as an instance of the unique number three. The Platonic solution was to posit an idea of three in which any three units would have to participate. These Ideal Numbers of Plato, critiqued by Aristotle in his *Metaphysics,* were qualities rather than quantities and as such could be neither operated with nor arranged in a sequence (Klein 1992). Compare with the following 1933 piece by Kharms:

> Numbers do not exist in a sequence. No number needs to be surrounded by other numbers. We distinguish between the arithmetical relations of numbers and their natural relations. The arithmetical sum of numbers produces a new number, whereas the natural union of numbers does not produce a new number. There is no equality in nature. There are identity, correspondence, representation, difference, and opposition. Nature does not equate one thing with another. Two

trees cannot equal each other. They can be equal in their length, in their width, and, generally, in all their properties. But as two natural wholes two trees cannot equal each other. Many people think that numbers are quantitative concepts abstracted from nature. We, however, think that numbers constitute a real species. We think that numbers are like trees or like grass. But while trees are subject to the action of time, numbers never change. Time and space do not influence numbers. Immutability allows numbers to be the laws of other things.

When we say *two*, We do not intend that to mean *one and one more*. When, above, we said *two trees*, we were using one of the properties of *two* and closing our eyes to all of its other properties. *Two trees* meant that we were talking about one tree and one more tree. In this case *two* expressed only quantity and was located in the number series, or, as We think, in the number wheel, between the one and the three.

The number wheel has its own way of formation. It is formed from a rectilinear figure denominated *the cross*. (Kharms 2004, 314–15.)

90   *Kozma Prutkov registered the world from the Assay Office . . .* The product of a mid-nineteenth-century literary mystification, the poet and bureaucrat Kozma Prutkov was claimed by Kharms as a literary ancestor.

90   *Khlebnikov* Velimir Khlebnikov's brochure *Time, the Measure of the World*, published in 1916, expounded his mathematical theory of the periodicity of history, subsequently developed in his *Tables of Destiny*. For the influence of Khlebnikov, characterized by Lipavsky as "the first to discover the wave structure of the world" (Sazhin et al. 1998, 1:187), on the *chinars*, see Kobrinskii 2000, 1:99–188. Khlebnikov appears as a character in Kharms's play *Lapa*, available in English translation by Matvei Yankelevich (Kharms 2001), and in Zabolotsky's "Triumph of Agriculture."

Notnow

The act of distinguishing between *this* and *that* is the first step of thought in *chinar* philosophy. "Notnow" may be regarded as an example of a *cisfinite* procedure (see note to "To Ring—To Fly").

To Ring—To Fly

According to Jaccard, Kharms's concept of *cisfinitum* (this side of the finite) refers to the qualitative state of the world before it is broken into pieces by reason through, for instance, the application of numbers whether finite or transfinite. *Cisfinite* logic, not subject to the laws of identity, contradiction, and excluded middle, describes things as free of relations: this is why they soar. (Jaccard 1991, 109–19; also Sazhin et al. 1998, 2:635.)

The World

Another example of *cisfinite* procedure, "The World" bears the title *Myr* in the original, combining the word for "world" (*mir*) with the word for "we" (*my*).

An Evening Song to She Who Exists by My Name

The open-ended metaphor or "hieroglyph" of the window had special significance for Kharms, since he converted it into a monogram of his first wife, Esther Rusakova (1909–43), the poem's dedicatee.

The Daughter of Patruliov

The original is untitled.

Before Coming to See You

The original is untitled.

Fenorov in America

The original is untitled.

Anton Antonovich Shaved Off His Beard

The original is untitled.

On the Death of Kazimir Malevich

Malevich died on May 15, 1935. His funeral was the last public manifestation of the Leningrad avant-garde. Lydia Ginzburg writes: "They buried

Malevich to music and in a Suprematist coffin. People lined the Nevsky like tapestries, and in the crowds it was said that it must be some foreigner they were burying. . . . The Suprematist coffin was realized according to a drawing by the departed. He had wanted for a square, a circle, and a cross to go on the lid, but he was denied the cross, even though he had called it an intersection of two planes" (Ginzburg 1999, 148, Ostashevsky's translation). Kharms read this poem during the funeral service. Despite the genuineness of his grief, and despite the striking concordance of the piece with Malevich's late work, the rough draft was not addressed to Malevich at all, but possibly to Oleinikov. (See variants in Meilakh et al. 1994, 564–65.)

One Fat Man

The original is untitled.

The Blue Notebook

Kharms was an avid diarist and note-taker, two volumes of his notes being recently published in Russia as *Zapisnye knizhki* (Kharms 2002). Lying halfway between the imaginative and the documentary, the so-called Blue Notebook (the original is untitled) demonstrates Kharms's refusal to distinguish between life and art.

128 *There lived a redheaded man* In the margin of the piece about the redheaded man, Kharms wrote: "Against Kant." He used the piece again in his "Incidences."

134 *Zhitkov* Boris Zhitkov (1882–1938), children's writer.

134 *Marina* Marina Malich, Kharms's second wife.

135 *This is how hunger begins* See note to "A Man Once Walked Out of His House" on the next page.

One Man Fell Asleep

The original is untitled.

137   *poods*   A pood equals 40 Russian pounds or 36.11 pounds US. The pounds in the translation are Russian.

A Magazine Article

Intended for Kharms's private magazine *Tapir*, of which only the prospectus and this article appear to have been finished.

138   *Teniers*   The paintings of David Teniers the Younger (1610–94) are well represented in the Hermitage Museum in St. Petersburg. According to Sazhin (Kharms 2000–1, 4:105), Kharms is alluding to Teniers's "Village Festival" and "Kermiss."

A Man Once Walked Out of His House

This poem came out in the children's magazine the *Finch* when the 1937 purge was in full swing. It was therefore suspected of being an allegory of disappearances. At the Children's State Publishing House, wrote Kharms in his diary, "They found something wrong with my poems. Now they're out to get me. They stopped publishing me. They stopped paying me, but they say the money is getting held up accidentally. I know there's something secret and evil happening there. We have nothing to eat. We are literally starving. I know this is the end. I am now going to the publishing house, so that they can again refuse me the money" (Kharms 2002, 2:192, Ostashevsky's translation). It should be said that many arrests were made at Kharms's publishing house that year and that he got off easy, considering. A year later, his children's poems started again getting into print.

How I Was Visited by Messengers

Written in response to Druskin's letter on p. 236. For *messengers*, see the introduction to this volume, p. xxvii.

Passacaglia 1

143   *passacaglia*   "A musical form of the seventeenth and eighteenth centuries consisting of continuous variations on a ground bass" (*American Heritage Dictionary*). Bach, the favorite composer of Kharms and Druskin, wrote passacaglias.

143 *Hoffmann* The German writer E. T. A. Hoffmann (1776–1822) specialized in the supernatural.

Maltonius Olbren

Of all *chinar* concepts, the miracle is one most closely associated with Kharms. Starting as the breaking of natural law, the concept later acquired the deeper significance of inner transformation: I am now free because I realize that natural law depends on my agreement to observe it. The miracle maker in Kharms's "Old Woman" dies without having performed a single miracle (Kharms and Vvedensky 1997, 123–54; Kharms 1993, 17–46). Kharms claimed to have witnessed the artist Vladimir Tatlin hover six inches above the ground during a successful experiment in personal levitation (Jaccard 1991, 124–30).

The Four-Legged Crow

The text parodies Ivan Krylov's adaptation of La Fontaine's adaptation of Aesop's "The Fox and the Cheese." Due to the popularity of Krylov's fable, "crow" in Russian slang has grown to mean something like "sucker." Hence the fox's insult is an intertextual joke.

The Adventure of Katerpillar

Katerpillar's name was originally transcribed from the English "caterpillar." There is no mention of Kafka's *Metamorphosis* in Kharms's surviving notebooks.

Nikolai Zabolotsky

Nikolai Zabolotsky (1903–58), the son of an agronomist, moved to Petrograd as a student. In 1929 he became the only member of OBERIU to publish a book of poems, *Stolbtsy* (*Columns*). The poems in our anthology date from 1929 to 1933, because the translator considered them closer to OBERIU-*chinar* thought, despite the fact that Zabolotsky was by then drifting away from the group. Scheduled for publication in 1933, his second book was kept from print because of the invective that met the appearance of "The Triumph of Agriculture" in *Zvezda* magazine. Critics read the poem—needless to say, incorrectly—as a satire of Soviet agricultural policy, especially collectivization. After 1933, Zabolotsky moved toward more traditional forms, adding a substantial body of lyrical nature poetry to his achievements. A biography of Zabolotsky by his son Nikita Zabolotsky has appeared in English (Zabolotsky 1994).

The Triumph of Agriculture

Although our anthology includes only about half of this piece, it is enough to provide the reader with a sense of the author's strange utopianism. Zabolotsky was a fan of pioneering scientists such as the geologist Vladimir Vernadsky, who coined the term "biosphere"; the botanist Kliment Timiriazev, who wondered whether plants may be said to be endowed with consciousness; and Konstantin Tsiolkovsky, the founder of rocketry and theorist of space travel (Zabolotsky 1994). The poet believed the mission of humankind was to alleviate the hard lot of lower life forms, especially of animals. "The Triumph of Agriculture" prophesies that Communism, collectivization, and future science will free animals from exploitation and disease, rendering them happier and more rational.

161   *"a vision of a cheerless graveyard"*   Zabolotsky is describing the grave of Velimir Khlebnikov, whose lines "I see horse-freedom / and equal rights for cows" gave the initial impetus for "The Triumph of Agriculture." The lines are from the poem "Ladomir," available in English as "Lightland" in Khlebnikov 1987–98, 3:168–82. Excerpts from *The Tables of Destiny* also may be found in Khlebnikov 1987–98, 2:417–33.

163   *kulak*   "Kulak" is a derogatory term for a prosperous peasant, deriving from the word for "fist." The word was much bandied about in the twenties and the thirties when any peasant resisting the policy of forced collectivization, adopted by the Central Committee in November 1928, was branded as such (no matter his true economic status). By 1937 literally millions of the so-called kulaks had been arrested, herded into cattle cars, and imprisoned in the camps or resettled in the underdeveloped areas of the Soviet Union. The total human cost of collectivization has been estimated

at 14.5 million, with five million deaths alone due to the 1932–33 famine in the Ukraine (Conquest 1987).

The Test of the Will

The name Korneev derives from the Russian for "root" (*koren'*), while Agafonov is from the Greek for "good." Agafon was also the name of Zabolotsky's grandfather.

Nikolai Oleinikov

Nikolai Oleinikov (1898–1937), born in a Cossack family, fought for the Reds during the civil war, joining the Party in 1920. He relocated to Leningrad in 1925 to embark on a career in children's literature at what became the Children's State Publishing House. In 1928, he invited the poets of OBERIU to write for his new magazine, the *Hedgehog,* where he performed the arduously double function of chief editor and hero of comic book. A master of practical jokes, toasts, and improvisations, Oleinikov conceived of his poetry as "party poetry," the kind of foray into cliché that may be described, with Run-DMC, as "not *bad* meaning bad, but *bad* meaning good." His many poetic personae included not only those of incorrigible womanizer, epicurean, and moralist but also those of natural scientist and mathematician, in clear parody of OBERIU-*chinar* interests. Oleinikov's manuscripts on number theory and philosophy of mathematics were confiscated during his arrest.

In Service of Science

"I'm on a mission to outperform my competition," parodies the Soviet-speak of industrialization and the five year plan, namely, the calls to increase productivity through enthusiasm-based "socialist competition." In preparing this poem for publication, Oleinikov self-censored this line to read: "I am developing a philosophy of the world" (Oleinikov 2000, 236, Ostashevsky's translation).

To a Lady Unwilling to Renounce Consumption of Meat from Cherkassy

Cherkassy is a city in Ukraine that is famous for its beef. According to Aleksandr Oleinikov, the poem mocks the rabbit-breeding campaign of

1932, which mandated the raising of rabbits in state institutions as a measure against beef shortages (Oleinikov 2000, 236).

For the Recovery of Heinrich

Poem addressed to Genrikh Levin (1903–71), art editor of children's magazines the *Hedgehog* and the *Finch*.

Zeros

Kharms, for whom zero was the basis of his cisfinite number system, also wrote several texts on the same topic.

Leonid Lipavsky

Leonid Lipavsky (1904–41), born in a family of Petersburg Jews, became friends with Vvedensky in high school and subsequently wrote children's literature under the pseudonym of Leonid Saveliev. His real calling was philosophy. Kharms once described him as "the theoretician of the *chinars*." He suggested such key *chinar* concepts as hieroglyph, messenger, and neighboring world. In 1931, he married Vvedensky's ex-girlfriend—and their mutual former schoolmate—Tatiana Meier.

Water Tractatus

In the work of the *chinars*, the hieroglyph of water almost always implicates time. The translator opted to keep some of the manuscript idiosyncrasies of the "Water Tractatus," such as the switch into "we" in the beginning of the Champion's Tale. It is unclear whether the unattributed lines on pages 209–10 are spoken by any of the characters. Some kind of diagram was meant to replace the word "cylinder" on page 215.

Yakov Druskin

Yakov Druskin (1902–80) attended the same high school as Vvedensky and Lipavsky. After his university degree in philosophy, he took classes at the Leningrad Conservatory, from which he graduated in 1929 with a degree as a pianist. In 1938 he got his third degree, in mathematics. Unlike the rest of the *chinars*, he did not write for children but made his living as a schoolteacher, first of literature, then of math. Druskin was an original and deeply religious philosopher. The introspective Christian existentialism that he developed did not contradict his Jewish origins—and his refusal to be baptized—in Leningrad as much as it would have in the West. He saved Kharms's, Vvedensky's, and many of Oleinikov's writings from disappearance in the first and worst winter of the blockade of Leningrad. Apart from philosophical essays and diaries, his own writings include published studies of Bach and astounding analyses of Vvedensky. For more Druskin in English, see Epstein 1998.

Death

This essay, excerpted from Druskin's diaries (Druskin 1999–2001, 1:55–66), is dedicated to the death of his father Simon (Shimel-Mordukh), a medical doctor.

220   *peccadillo*   Druskin invented the *chinar* phrase "a certain equilibrium with a slight peccadillo" in 1933. Its meaning is deliberately vague, but the peccadillo is, as it were, departure from dead symmetry by either aleatory or voluntary error that constitutes creation in both the cosmological and the artistic senses of the word.

220   *Lida*   The philosopher's sister Lidia.

222   *Pushkin*   A suburb of Leningrad, formerly known as Tsarskoe and subsequently Detskoe Selo (until 1937, which indicates revision of diary). Druskin alternates between "Pushkin" and "Detskoe." I opted to keep "Pushkin" throughout for greater clarity.

223   *Tiutchev*   Fedor Tiutchev, Russian Romantic poet (1803–73); the allusion is to his poem "Twins."

226   *Leonid Andreev*   Russian writer (1871–1919); the allusion is to his story "Eliazar."

230   *Lipavsky*   In the original noted by letter *L*.

232   *coastal dwellers*   Allusion to Druskin's tractate "On the Happy Life" (1934).

234   *Georg*   Leonid Georg was the Russian literature teacher at the high school where Druskin, Lipavsky, and Vvedensky met. In the original noted by letter *G*.

Letter to Kharms

The original is untitled. See note to Kharms's "How I Was Visited by Messengers" and our introduction, p. xxvii.

The End of the World

The untitled original forms part of Druskin's diaries (Druskin 1999–2001, 1:86–87).

Bakhterev, Igor. 1977. "Kogda my byli molodymi." In *Vospominaniia o Zabolotskom*. Moscow: Sovetskii pisatel'.

Charms, Daniil. 1992. *Fälle: Szenen, Gedichte, Prosa*. Translated by Peter Urban. Berlin: Friedenauer Presse.

———. 2003. *Disastri*. Translated by Paolo Nori. Turin: Einaudi.

Conquest, Robert. 1968. *The Great Terror: Stalin's Purge of the Thirties*. New York: Macmillan.

———. 1987. *The Harvest of Sorrow: Soviet Collectivization and the Terror-Famine*. Cambridge: Oxford University Press.

Druskin, Yakov. 1999–2001. *Dnevniki*. 2 vols. St. Petersburg: Akademicheskii proekt.

Epstein, Thomas. 1998. "The 'Unofficial' Life and Thoughts of Iakov Semenovich Druskin." *Symposion* 3:1–28.

Fink, Hilary L. 1999. *Bergson and Russian Modernism, 1900–1930*. Evanston, IL: Northwestern University Press.

Florenskii, Pavel. 1994–98. *Sochineniia*, 4 vols. Moscow: Mysl'.

Gerasimova, Anna. n.d. "Bednyi vsadnik, ili Pushkin bez golovy." http://www.umka.ru/liter/930602.html.

Ginzburg, Lidia. 1999. *Zapisnye knizhki*. Moscow: Zakharov.

Harms, Daniil. 1993. *Écrits*. Translated by Jean-Philippe Jaccard. Paris: Christian Bourgois.

Henderson, Linda Dalrymple. 1983. *The Fourth Dimension and Non-Euclidean Geometry in Modern Art*. Princeton, NJ: Princeton University Press.

Iampol'skii, Mikhail. 1998. *Bespamiatsvo kak istok: Chitaia Kharmsa*. Moscow: NLO.

Jaccard, Jean-Philippe. 1991. *Daniil Harms et la fin de l'avant-garde russe*. Slavica Helvetica 39. Bern: Peter Lang.

Janecek, Gerald. 1996. *Zaum: The Transrational Poetry of Russian Futurism*. San Diego, CA: San Diego State University Press.

Kharms, Daniil. 1978–88. *Sobraniie proizvedenii.* Edited by M. B. Meilakh and Vladimir Erl'. 4 vols. Bremen: K-Presse.

―――. 1993. *Incidences.* Translated by Neil Cornwell. London: Serpent's Tail.

―――. 2000–1. *Sobraniie sochinenii.* 4 vols. Edited by V. N. Sazhin. St. Petersburg: Azbuka.

―――. 2001. "Lapa." Translated by Matvei Yankelevich, with preface by Branislav Jakovljevic. *PAJ: A Journal of Performance and Art* 68 (May 2001) 23:2:75–104.

―――. 2002. *Zapisnye knizhki.* Edited by V. N. Sazhin and J.-Ph. Jaccard. 2 vols. St. Petersburg: Akademicheskii proekt.

―――. 2004. *O iavleniiakh i suschestvovaniiakh.* St. Petersburg: Azbukaklassika.

―――. *See also* Charms, Daniil *and* Harms, Daniil.

Kharms, Daniil, and Alexander Vvedensky. 1997. *The Man with the Black Coat: Russia's Literature of the Absurd.* Translated by George Gibian. Evanston, IL: Northwestern University Press. (Orig. pub. as *Russia's Lost Literature of the Absurd* [Ithaca, NY: Cornell University Press, 1971].)

Khlebnikov, Velimir. 1987–98. *Collected Works.* Translated by Paul Schmidt. 3 vols. Cambridge, MA: Harvard University Press.

Klein, Jacob. 1992. *Greek Mathematical Thought and the Origin of Algebra.* Translated by Eva Brann. New York: Dover.

Kobrinskii, A. A. 2000. *Poetika "OBERIU" v kontekste russkogo literaturnogo avangarda.* 2nd ed. 2 vols. Moscow: Izdatel'stvo Moskovskogo kul'turologicheskogo litseia.

Levin, Ilya. 1978. "The Fifth Meaning of the Motor-Car: Malevich and the *Oberiuty.*" *Soviet Union/Union Soviétique* 5 (2): 287–300.

Mal'skii, I. 1992. "Razgrom OBERIU: Materialy sledstvennogo dela." *Oktiabr,* November, 166–91.

Meilakh, M. B. 1991a. "Oberiuty i zaum'." In *Zaumnyi futurizm i dadaizm v russkoi kul'ture.* Edited by Luigi Magarotto, Marzio Marzaduri, and Daniella Rizzi, 361–75. Ricerche di cultura europea 2. Bern: Peter Lang.

―――. 1991b. "Zametki o teatre oberiutov." *Teatr* 11 (November): 173–79.

―――. 1998. "Gibel' Aleksandra Vvedenskogo," 567–83. *Tynianovskii sbornik. Vypusk desiatyi: shestye, sed'mye, vos'mye Tynianovskiie chteniia.* Moscow.

Meilakh, M. B., V. I. Erl', T. L. Nikol'skaia, and A. N. Oleinikov, eds. 1994. *Poety gruppy OBERIU.* Biblioteka poeta. St. Petersburg: Sovetskii pisatel'.

Nakhimovsky, Alice Stone. 1982. *An Introduction to the Writings of Daniil Kharms and Alexander Vvedenski.* Wiener Slawistischer Almanach. Special vol. 5. Vienna.

Oleinikov, Nikolai. 2000. *Stikhotvoreniia i poemy.* Novaia biblioteka poeta. St. Petersburg: Akademicheskii proekt.

Platt, Kevin. 2003. "N. A. Zabolotskii and the Stalinist Sublime." In *Strannaia poeziia i strannaia proza: Filologicheskii sbornik, posviaschennyi 100-letiu so dnia rozhdeniia N. A. Zabolotskogo.* Noveishie issledovaniia russkoi kul'tury 3. Moscow: Piataia strana.

Roberts, Graham. 1997. *The Last Soviet Avant-Garde: OBERIU—Fact, Fiction, Metafiction.* Cambridge: Cambridge University Press.

Rosenthal, Bernice Glatzer, ed. 1995. *Neo-Kantianism in Russian Thought.* Special issue of *Studies in East European Thought* 47, no. 3–4 (December): 151–294.

Sazhin, V. N. 1990. "Sborishche druzei, ostavlennykh sud'boiu." *Tynianovskii sbornik: Chetvertye Tynianovskiie chteniia.* Riga: Zinatne.

———. 2004. *A. Vvedenskii i D. Kharms v ikh perepiske.* Bibliograf 18. Paris: Russkii Institut v Parizhe.

Sazhin, V. N., L. S. Druskina, and A. G. Mashevskii, eds. 1998. *"Sborishche druzei, ostavlennykh sud'boiu." A. Vvedenskii, L. Lipavskii, Ia. Druskin, D. Kharms, N. Oleinikov: "Chinari" v tekstakh, dokumentakh i issledovaniiakh.* 2 vols. Moscow: privately printed.

Sidney, Sir Philip. 1963. *The Defence of Poesie: Political Discourses, Correspondence, Translation.* Cambridge: Cambridge University Press.

Todd, Albert C., and Max Hayward, eds. 1993. *Silver and Steel: Twentieth-Century Russian Poetry.* New York: Doubleday.

Tokarev, D. V. 2002. *Kurs na khudshee: Absurd kak kategoria teksta u D. Kharmsa i S. Bekketa.* Moscow: NLO.

Ustinov, Andrei. 1990. "Delo Detskogo sektora Gosizdata 1932 goda," 125–36. In *Mikhail Kuzmin i russkaia kul'tura XX veka.* Leningrad: Muzei Akhmatovoi.

Vvedenski, Alexandre. 2002. *Oeuvres complètes.* Translated by Jacques Burko, Madeleine Lejeune, and Christine Zeytounian-Beloüs. Paris: Éditions de la Différence.

Vvedenskii, Aleksandr. 1980–84. *Polnoie sobraniie sochinenii.* Edited by M. B. Meilakh. 2 vols. Ann Arbor, MI: Ardis.

———. 1993. *Polnoie sobraniie proizvedenii.* 2 vols. Edited by M. B. Meilakh and V. I. Erl'. Moscow: Gileia.

Vvedenskij, Aleksandr. 1986. *Kuprijanov und Nataša.* Translated by Peter Urban. Berlin: Friedenauer Presse.

Vvedensky, Alexander. 2002. *The Gray Notebook.* Translated by Matvei Yankelevich. New York: Ugly Duckling Presse.

Zabolotskii, N. A. 2002. *Polnoie sobraniie stikhotvorenii i poem.* Novaia biblioteka poeta. St. Petersburg: Akademicheskii proekt.

Zabolotsky, Nikita. 1994. *The Life of Zabolotsky.* Translated by R. R. Milner-Gulland and C. G. Bearne. Cardiff: University of Wales Press.

Zabolotsky, Nikolay. 1999. *Selected Poems.* Translated by Daniel Weissbort. Manchester: Carcanet.